About the Authors

Ross Perot is founder of the Reform Party, United We Stand America, Perot Systems, and Electronic Data Systems. He is the recipient of numerous honors, including, *The Horatio Alger Award, The National Business Hall of Fame Award, The Winston Churchill Award, The Patrick Henry Award,* and *The Raoul Wallenberg Award.* Mr. Perot received 19.7 million votes in the 1992 presidential election.

Senator Paul Simon served in the U.S. House of Representatives for ten years before being elected to the U.S. Senate in 1984. Senator Simon, the author of fifteen books, introduced the Balanced Budget Amendment in 1986, and it has been the cornerstone of the balanced budget debate since that time.

The Dollar Crisis

The Dollar Crisis

A Blueprint To Help Rebuild The American Dream

Ross Perot
and U.S. Senator
Paul Simon

THE SUMMIT PUBLISHING GROUP

THE SUMMIT PUBLISHING GROUP
One Arlington Centre, 1112 East Copeland Road, Fifth Floor
Arlington, Texas 76011

Printed in the United States of America.

00 99 98 97 96   040   5 4 3 2 1

ISBN 1-56530-217-6

Cover and book design by David Sims

Contents

Acknowledgments

This book reflects countless hours of research by three individuals dedicated to educating the American public. The authors would like to thank Mike Poss, Marvin Singleton, and David Chiu for making complex subjects easier to understand.

Introduction

Each year, nearly fifty thousand new books are published. Some entertain, some teach, and a few, including this one, attempt to change the world. Of course, to some this might seem to be an implausible goal—but that, indeed, is the reason we are presenting our recommendations for a better America on the following pages.

The main message that we want to convey is that we cannot continue on our present course. We, like the prodigal son, have inherited a great treasure and have squandered it by living beyond our means as a nation. Unlike the prodigal, unfortunately, we have no benign benefactor who will make all things economically right again. No, we must solve the difficulties we have created for ourselves—**and the time to do so is now**.

Our first intention is to explore how money and currencies were created, and why. We will then address how imprudent management of that money can cause an entire nation to become weak politically, economically, and socially. Specifically, this book details the dangers facing us if we don't adopt economic policies that will bolster world-wide confidence in the United States, our people, and our currency.

Fortunately, the problem is not yet out of control—we can still pass on to future generations the bounty of our great land. But the opportunity to do so is rapidly slipping away. The signs of peril are there. Budget and trade deficits are on the verge of choking the United States economy, and her citizens are watching in disbelief as their quality of life diminishes annually.

To halt this decline, the federal budget must be balanced. The trade deficit must be erased. Citizens must bolster their savings, and our nation must focus on doing what's right over decades and not be content with short-term solutions.

Yes, there are ways to preserve the United States in its role of prominence and dignity in the global arena. It is our purpose here to identify potential solutions and then to challenge the reader to act upon them—to raise the quality of life for ourselves and for generations to come—in a nutshell, to change the world.

Part One

What's the Problem?

"No country can devalue its way to prosperity."

LARRY SUMMERS
Assistant Secretary of the Treasury

Chapter 1

The Zloty and the American Dream

Not too many centuries ago, people purchased commodities primarily with other commodities. For example, a bottle of wine might have bought a bushel of wheat. A person who knew how to make a table and chairs out of a log could barter those items for food or clothing. Nations traded with other nations in much the same way. Gradually, gold, diamonds, and other precious stones and rare metals became a more convenient way of acquiring goods from other nations or from merchants in faraway ports.

Eventually, national currencies were developed. Coins were used early on, and later paper became accepted. Today, a check is a form of currency. When you write the check, you do it with the understanding that your "faith and credit" back it. A system based on trust works well as long as everyone is honest. However, people quickly lose confidence in someone who writes checks that are not worth any more than the paper on which they are printed. Eventually, they will refuse to deal with those who don't make good on their IOUs.

The same is true on a global basis. Nations issue paper currency with different names: dollar, yen, deutsche mark, pound, franc, lire, and many others. Those pieces of paper, like your check, carry the implied promise that they have the "full faith and credit" of a particular country. As with a bad check, people and nations gradually lose confidence in any country whose currency does not maintain its value.

Most trade within a nation and between nations is done with currency, or it is at least designated in currency terms. In America, farmers sell their food products for dollars, as do car dealers, pharmacists, and computer software developers. When trade is conducted with another nation, it is done with the explicit understanding that the purchaser will pay in a specified currency. Sometimes there is an agreement that if the designated currency depreciates in value between the date the contract is signed and the date of payment, an adjustment will be made.

A currency is described as *stable* when it is dependable, constant, and trustworthy. Stable currencies help facilitate world trade. Unstable currencies hinder trade between countries by introducing uncertainty into a transaction that is probably already complicated by its international setting. Business transactions across national borders total almost a trillion dollars a day, and because of the stability of the currencies used, those transactions can be consummated in seconds.

But the process has its complexities. Currency value fluctuations can have short-term consequences for the people of a nation whose currency has changed. As a minor example, a magazine promotion on television recently advertised that a subscription for one year was available for eighteen dollars to U.S. viewers but twenty-three dollars (Canadian) for Canadian viewers. The same subscription had been available to Canadian viewers for twenty-one dollars (Canadian) a few years earlier, even while the price was then eighteen dollars (U.S.). Because Canada's dollar has depreciated more rapidly than the U.S. dollar, that magazine subscription price is a small penalty Canadians must pay for the fiscal policies of their government. On a larger scale, consider the adverse implications for a country when a company hesitates to proceed with a project because of the uncertainty caused by excessive currency fluctuations. Jobs that might have been brought to a country can easily go to another nation with a more stable currency simply because the investment risk is lower in the country with the stable currency.

As in the example above, the value of the U.S. dollar—like the stock market—goes up and down each day relative to other currencies. Sometimes there is an upward swing and sometimes a downward trend, but the long-term tendency has been down.

That is illustrated, unfortunately, by the fact that confidence in U.S. currency—the dollar—has slipped over the years, and that lack of faith adversely affects the quality of life for most Americans. To say that "A dollar doesn't go as far as it used to," may be a cliché, but it is reality for every one of us. Fortunately, just as imprudent policies of the past have caused the dollar to drop in value, wiser policies can improve the situation.

This point is dramatically exemplified by the recent situation in Poland, whose currency is the zloty. During the Communist era in that country, it was almost worthless. Americans visiting Poland found upon their return to the United States that banks would not convert the Polish currency into dollars. Even businesses at the Warsaw airport would not accept payment for anything in zlotys. They accepted dollars, deutsche marks, or other relatively stable currencies, but not their own. Since the demise of the Polish Communist government in 1989, sensible fiscal and monetary policies have been followed. Today, the zloty is a respected currency. This recognition has helped bring significant investment to Poland and a visible rise in the standard of living of many of her people.

The daily fluctuations in currency values may seem almost irrelevant to some of us. And the fact that the numbers reflecting those values are buried in small print deep in newspapers only tends to minimize their importance. Nothing could be farther from the truth, however. Those vital statistics reflect major shifts of confidence and, therefore, value among currencies of the world. In turn, those changes of value determine how much the citizens of those countries pay for everything from electricity, to food, to cars, to clothes. In other words, fluctuations in those numbers foretell substantial adjustments in the lives of people all over the globe.

Speaking of fluctuations, do you remember when people around the world frequently used the phrase, "the almighty dollar"? Those words are not used as often as they once were, are they? And if we do not take decisive action soon, we will hear them even less frequently as the stability of, and confidence in, the United States dollar erodes.

Americans want to feel financially secure. It is a legitimate part of the American dream. But we cannot have it with an unstable dollar, and we cannot have a stable dollar unless we make some changes.

Chapter 2

Where Have We Been and Where Should We Go?

anish philosopher Søren Kierkegaard said: "Life must be lived forwards but can only be understood backwards." This statement is also true of national and international finance. To understand where we should go, we must first understand where we have been.

From the Past to the Present

The ancient city-state of Lydia issued the first guaranteed currency in approximately 680 A.D. when its government created official coins. The advent of currency proved to be a great boost to trade, and the Greeks soon followed the Lydian example with coins minted on the island of Aegina. Soon, every nation in the Mediterranean region had its own currency. Historian Will Durant tells us that the introduction of currency "had effects as momentous and interminable as those that came from the introduction of the alphabet."

Coins were a combination of gold and lesser metals, which were used to harden the coins and make them more durable. It wasn't long before nations figured out that they could cut the cost of minting coins by "debasing" their currencies. The procedure for debasing a currency simply involves increasing the proportion of the common metal and decreasing the proportion of the precious metal contained in a coin. Durant notes:

> *Every city [state] has its own individual coinage...Every Greek government, except the Athenian, cheats by debasing its coins...The Athenian government, from Solon onward, helps Athenian trade powerfully by establishing a reliable coinage, stamped with the owl of Athens.*

So, problems of devaluing the currency are not new.

Other nations developed different means for facilitating trade. Rock salt became the currency in Abyssinia, and whale teeth were used in the Fiji Islands.

Eighteenth Century

Paper money, as we know it, is a relatively recent development. In the American colonies, individual governments and land banks issued notes called *bills of credit*. However, the Revolutionary War created a major financial problem for our future nation. Congress and the states issued bonds, notes, and other pieces of paper, backed in theory by gold, to attempt to pay for the war. But as debts rose, the temptation grew to "solve" the debt problem by issuing more and more paper, worth less and less. Putting more paper money into circulation debases a currency as surely as changing the metallic content of a country's coinage. The flood of paper money resulted in massive inflation after the Revolution, with the currency averaging about *one dollar in gold or silver value for each $167 in paper*!

Our early leaders learned a lesson the hard way. When James Madison and others wrote our Constitution, they authorized the federal government to coin money and prohibited the states from doing so. Our first secretary of the Treasury, Alexander Hamilton, developed a system for eliminating the federal debt. But for a few years in the 1790s, more than 40 percent of the expenditures of the new government went for interest payments— even worse than our record today. A few years after the Revolutionary War, John Adams wrote to Thomas Jefferson:

> *All the perplexities, confusions and distresses in America arise, not from defects in their [sic] constitution or confederation, not from a want*

of honor or virtue, so much as from downright
ignorance of coin, credit and circulation.

Meanwhile, states and banks continued to issue notes.

Nineteenth Century

The British dramatically restricted the rights of their banks to issue notes in 1844. In 1863, the U.S. Congress passed the National Bank Act that also restricted—but did not ban—the ability of banks in the United States to issue notes. During the Civil War, the federal government issued more than $150 million in "greenbacks"—notes backed by the United States government. Our currency to this day remains green, unlike the multicolored currencies of many nations.

Both the Union and the Confederacy had great difficulty financing the Civil War. Union Treasury notes gradually dropped in their gold value to about fifty cents on the dollar by the end of the conflict. Not surprisingly, the Confederate dollar dropped to less than two cents of its original value. Just as in the aftermath of the Revolutionary War, inflation appeared in the post-Civil War era as a result of the proliferation of paper notes with limited value.

The federal government created a national currency for the first time in 1864, but it wasn't until

1879 that the currency was officially backed by gold. Congress authorized the minting of silver coins in the same year. The coins were issued in these denominations: three cents, fifteen cents, twenty-five cents, and fifty cents. In 1880, the federal government issued gold and silver certificates. However, it wasn't until 1913 that Congress established the Federal Reserve Board, the agency responsible for, among other things, monitoring the supply of coin and currency in circulation.

Twentieth Century

For most of the early part of this century, the British pound sterling was the dominant currency of international commerce. Great Britain had developed a sophisticated currency system well before the United States had an opportunity to grow and mature as a nation. The dominance of the British system reflected the military and political reality of that era. "The sun never sets on the British Empire," their leaders said with great pride. That statement reflected more than military and political dominance of colonies around the world. It also reflected the resources that Great Britain had at its disposal: gold from Rhodesia, cotton from India, and many other riches.

This far-reaching network gave substance and stability to the British currency and gave confidence to traders who used the pound to buy and sell commodities around the world. Because the value of any currency is ultimately based on the trust that investors and traders place in it, the value of the pound sterling reflected the confidence the world community placed in the British Empire.

Even though the United States had become the world's largest economy by the 1880s, Great Britain continued to play the dominant economic role until after World War I. British and European expenditures to finance the military buildup and the subsequent devastating war sapped their economic strength, and as a result, the world's gold reserves shifted more and more to the United States.

From 1880 until 1971, the United States generally backed the dollar with gold. But as the world's wealth, population, and productivity grew, it became clear that nations, including the United States, needed a more flexible means of determining the value of their currencies. But separating the value of currency from the value of gold raised the fundamental question that troubles every nation today: How is the needed currency flexibility achieved without succumbing to the temptation simply to print more money to meet immediate political needs or reduce onerous levels of growing debt?

Until recently, the federal government generally followed the advice of President George Washington in his farewell address, during which he advocated a policy of not acquiring debt. Throughout most of the history of the United States, there has been relatively little debt. In 1912, when Lawrence Chamberlain wrote his authoritative book, *The Work of the Bond House*, he devoted much more attention to railroad bonds, for example, than to Treasury bonds because the national debt was small and our currency was solid.

In 1934, however, President Franklin D. Roosevelt decreased the dollar from a value of $20.67 per ounce of gold to $35 per ounce and issued an executive order limiting the use of gold, stating that Americans could not export gold unless licensed to do so by the U.S. Treasury. Within days of that executive order, Monroe County, New York, advertised $350,000 in bonds with unprecedented language: "Both principal and interest payable in gold coin *or its equivalent in lawful money of the United States*" [italics added]. The italicized portion of the preceding sentence signaled the move away from the gold standard, which would be completed in 1971 with its final abandonment.

By the time of the 1971 abolishment of the gold standard, our reserves of gold had almost been depleted. In early 1961, President Dwight D. Eisenhower issued an executive order prohibiting Americans from purchasing and holding gold overseas. Not only did we have a problem with our gold reserve, the two largest gold-producing nations were the Soviet Union, whose political policies we abhorred, and South Africa, whose racial policies we found repugnant. Relying on gold as a basis for the currency, to many Americans, seemed to be playing into the hands of the Soviets and South Africans. Those two nations had the ability to manipulate the supply of gold for their own economic benefit.

Problems for the world's currencies were simmering but had not yet erupted. As late as 1968, President Lyndon B. Johnson told Congress in his State of the Union address:

We must strengthen the international monetary system. We have assured the world that America's full gold stock stands behind our commitment to maintain the price of gold at thirty-five dollars an ounce. We must back this commitment by legislating to free our gold reserves.

What he did not say was that our gold reserves were diminishing rapidly.

Three years later, in 1971, President Richard M. Nixon uncoupled the value of the dollar from the value of gold. This move barely preceded the first oil shock of 1973. The combination of those two events began a loss of confidence in both the dollar and the U.S. economy, initiating a round of inflation. When the second oil shock occurred in 1979, we had limited our ability to halt a worsening inflation rate.

The Vicious Cycle

The downward slide of the dollar since 1971 has not been caused by malice or intentional debauchery of the dollar. Instead, it is the result of expedient political actions taken by elected leaders in both parties, who believe the nation can somehow escape the following basic economic facts of life:

- Incurring too much debt weakens a nation.
- Printing too much money hurts a nation.
- Failing to develop policies that encourage savings has a penalty.
- Leaving too high a percentage of our population unlettered, unskilled, and unproductive has had unfavorable consequences.

Despite this emphasis on what has gone wrong with the U.S. economy, we have done some things correctly. For example, our one-dollar bill represents a much smaller unit of purchasing power than the smallest unit of German paper currency, which in November 1995 was worth about seven dollars. The smaller unit helps fluidity. We have almost no restriction on the movement of our currency, and that has added to its value. Our inflation record is not as good as that of a few nations, but it is better than most. Our system of colleges and universities is the best in the world, and it has added immensely to our productivity.

In any discussion of global economics, Japan's experience is instructive. Immediately after World War II, Japanese officials thought they could stimulate the economy of their battered nation by printing money. Their currency soon dropped to less than 1 percent of its pre-war value, and the financial markets, as a result, had a low regard for the Japanese currency. In an attempt to help, U.S. leaders sent a Detroit banker, Joseph Dodge, to Japan. He made a series of recommendations that Japan followed, and helped stabilize the currency at 360 yen to the dollar, where it stayed for almost twenty years. Dodge made other contructive suggestions which, in their desperation, the Japanese also accepted.

The tough economic medicine paid off. Today Japan is the No. 1 creditor nation in the world, while her benefactor, the United States, has failed to heed the advice that one of its own citizens gave to Japan and is now the No. 1 debtor nation in the world.

The reality of that fact is made apparent by sub-tracting the amount that other nations owe us from the amount that we owe other nations, which left the United States with a cumulative trade deficit of more than $1 trillion at the end of 1995. The following graph shows the astronomical rise in the deficit in the last ten years.

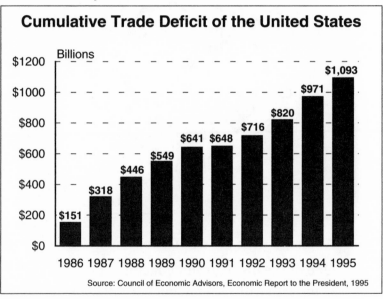

Cumulative Trade Deficit of the United States

Billions

$1,093
$971
$820
$716
$641 $648
$549
$446
$318
$151

1986 1987 1988 1989 1990 1991 1992 1993 1994 1995

Source: Council of Economic Advisors, Economic Report to the President, 1995

The dollar has fallen dramatically in value against the yen since 1971, and inflation is at least partly to blame for this decline. But, in turn, the drop in the dollar has added to inflation, which causes the value of the dollar to fall against the value of other currencies, and we're back to where we started. It's sort of the financial equivalent of discovering perpetual motion or cold fusion, but no one is trying to patent it. The following drawing describes this depreciating cycle.

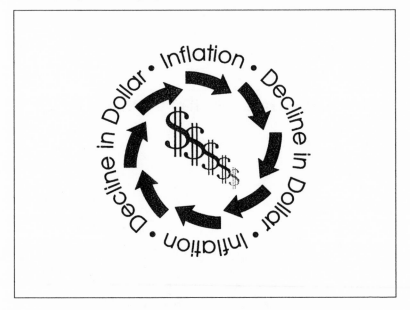

A Bumpy Ride for the Dollar

One of the distinguishing factors of the U.S. dollar compared with other major currencies is the role of inflation. During the last seventeen years, the U.S. inflation rate has exceeded that of Japan. The graph on the next page displays a four-decade analysis of the inflation rates of the United States and Japan as measured by the changes in the consumer price indexes for both countries.

A 1995 study for the Japan Economic Institute by Arthur Alexander concluded: "Higher rates of

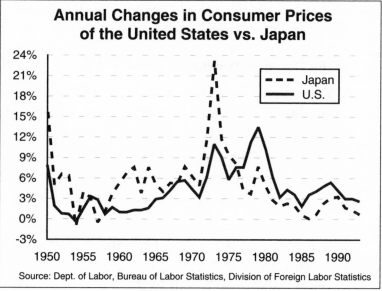

Annual Changes in Consumer Prices of the United States vs. Japan

Source: Dept. of Labor, Bureau of Labor Statistics, Division of Foreign Labor Statistics

inflation in the United States than in Japan account for about 65 percent of the change in the dollar-yen relationship over time."

Inflation takes its toll not only on the economy but also on presidential administrations. Hobart Rowen wrote of one presidency:

The central failure of the Carter Administration was its utter inability over four years to control inflation—a failure that would ultimately lead to the election of Ronald Reagan in 1980. Runaway inflation in the United States, at a time when authorities in Japan and Germany were able to keep prices under control, smashed

*global confidence in the dollar and encouraged
speculators to seek a safer haven in gold.*

The Dollar in Wartime

Toward the end of World War II, the United States
and other nations entered into the Bretton Woods
agreement to establish exchange rates for various
currencies. The most significant rate adopted by
the participating countries was the ten-year-old
rate of $35 per ounce of gold, used by the United
States as the value of the dollar. The theory
advanced by the leaders had merit: Stability in currencies would advance world trade. And for many
years, the Bretton Woods formula worked.

Historically, it has been shown that wartime sit-
uations strain the economies of the nations
involved. When the United States entered the
Korean War, President Harry S. Truman, to his great
credit, asked for a tax increase to pay for it. The
United States went through the conflict with few
major economic scars. But when we became mili-
tarily involved in Vietnam, President Johnson
understood that public support was not strong.
Rather than asking for an increase in taxes to pay
for our additional expenditures, he called for "a
unified budget," bringing the Social Security program and its sizable surplus into the budget. This
had the effect of producing a balanced budget,

thanks to the Social Security surplus. But having made the choice to play games with budget figures, the United States had unwittingly committed itself to an economically slippery slope.

The financial markets were not fooled. As we will see in the next chapter, when Johnson's successor, President Nixon, abandoned the gold standard in 1971, the dollar began its fall against the yen and most other major currencies.

The drop has not been a steady downhill slide. Like the stock market, currencies fluctuate in value. But having a dollar that is either too high or too low in value compared to other currencies is not good.

The United States, working through the Federal Reserve Board, can control the value of the dollar to some extent. When the value of the dollar is believed to be too high relative to the value of other currencies, the Federal Reserve can create more dollars, thereby lowering the value of the dollar. Conversely, if the value of the dollar is too low, the Federal Reserve can purchase dollars, thereby raising the value of the dollar. This process of controlling the value of the dollar is known as *intervention.*

The United States has purposely intervened from time to time to depress the value of the dollar. A significant intervention occurred during a meeting of financial leaders at the Plaza Hotel in New

York City on September 22, 1985. At that meeting, Treasury Secretary James Baker, supported by the highly respected but somewhat reluctant chairman of the Federal Reserve, Paul Volcker, persuaded the other major financial nations to devalue the dollar. Their aim was to increase U.S. exports through a lower dollar. It helped—temporarily.

The United States obviously has two international economic problems: the drop in the value of the dollar relative to the other two major currencies, the yen and the deutsche mark; and the instability of the dollar. These are not our problems alone. As a result of our significant impact on the rest of the world, all nations, to a greater or lesser extent, share in our fate, as do the citizens of each of those nations.

Chapter 3

Diagnosing the Problem

The once-stalwart United States dollar is in trouble. But, like many difficulties, the problem with the value of the dollar cannot be blamed on one factor. Economists seldom agree on anything, and there is certainly no consensus as to how the dollar reached its current status. Neither author of this book is an economist by training. But all of us are required to make economic decisions of one type or another throughout our lives. Those decisions we make every day are not greatly different (though much smaller in scale) than those that must be made by nations. The opinions offered throughout this book have been formed by the experiences of the authors in the business and political arenas over several decades. And while the general subject of this book concerns international currencies and exchange rates, those topics are analyzed with respect to their effects on the everyday lives of Americans.

The Gold Standard

Immediately after World War II, the United States accounted for more than half of the world's economy. By 1994, that proportion had dropped to a little more than 20 percent. Immediately after World War II, nations, businesses, and individuals who had dealings across national boundaries traded in U.S. dollars. People had confidence in the dollar. "It is as good as gold," U.S. leaders repeatedly said. And that was literally true—at that time, dollars could be exchanged for gold.

Many readers will remember that for decades, the dollar was pegged at the price of $35 per ounce of gold, as we described in the preceding chapter. A few readers also might recall the $20.67 price of an ounce of gold that was in effect from 1900 to January 1934. When President Roosevelt increased the price of gold to $35 per ounce in 1934, a youthful Dean Acheson was serving as secretary of the Treasury in place of the seriously ill William Woodfin. Acheson opposed FDR's financial actions and resigned in protest during what he described as "a spectacular row with the president." Acheson later became secretary of state in the Truman administration.

FDR's move to lower the value of the dollar to $35 for an ounce of gold dropped the value of the dollar in world markets. But the dollar remained at $35 per ounce until President Johnson's administration.

During the Johnson administration, the dollar technically remained at $35 per ounce of gold, but only foreign governments could receive gold in exchange for dollars. Banks and citizens could no longer buy gold at $35 an ounce. However, there was also an implicit agreement that other nations would not convert dollars into gold, for fear that it would destabilize the dollar. An unstable dollar was not in the best interest of any nation, because no other currency enjoyed the confidence level of the dollar at that time.

Finally, as we said earlier, the United States abandoned the gold standard in 1971 during the Nixon administration. But the earlier gold-to-dollar commitment, plus the buoyancy of the U.S. economy for an extended period, had given international leaders and financial markets a continuing confidence in the dollar.

Meanwhile, for decades many leaders of other countries privately had noted that their particular nations had more wealth than official statistics indicated. They usually were referring to the fact that some of their citizens had a portion of their wealth hidden away in the form of U.S. dollars. Most governments outlawed that practice because they wanted money to be invested and taxed at home. But no one anywhere questioned the value of Uncle Sam's dollar. As a result, the phrase "as sound as a dollar" became a favorite in languages around the world.

Within countries where the local currency was not sound, people often used U.S. currency as the means of trade. An American traveling virtually anywhere could pay for a taxi or a meal with dollars, even in nations that officially prohibited the practice. People everywhere were eager to get their hands on dollars. Today the dollar remains the most widely accepted currency in the world, but an American traveler is much more likely to need the currency of the foreign country he or she is visiting.

A Downward Trend

Unfortunately, times have changed. This is attributable to the growth in the economies of other nations as well as a slowing of U.S. growth. The following graph shows how other regions of the world have grown comparatively since 1960.

Obviously, we are still the world's economic giant. However, the instability created by our burgeoning $5 trillion national debt and the ongoing federal budget stalemate has eroded world confidence in the dollar.

For much of this century, the United States was the world's largest creditor nation. No other country was even close. But in the 1980s, that situation changed dramatically. We ignored our fiscal prob-

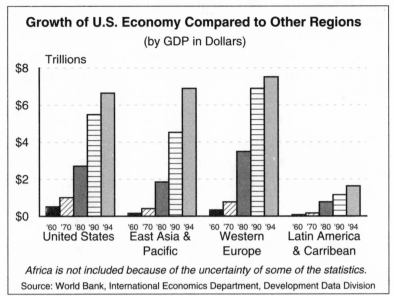

Growth of U.S. Economy Compared to Other Regions
(by GDP in Dollars)

Africa is not included because of the uncertainty of some of the statistics.

Source: World Bank, International Economics Department, Development Data Division

lems by allowing ourselves to live with an unbalanced federal budget, building a staggering national debt in the process. During the same time period, we became the world's largest debtor nation. In fact, we are the only industrialized nation in history to move from creditor to debtor status during peacetime. Just as our fiscal and monetary policies have wavered, so, too, has the dollar faltered.

During the spring of 1995, the dollar took a decisive drop in value against other major world currencies. As discussed in greater detail in chapter 5, this decline was attributed to the failure of the Senate, by one vote, to pass the Balanced Budget Amendment. Most of us learned about the shrinkage of the dollar from newspapers, television, and radio, but it seemed remote. The diminishing dollar was, perhaps, vaguely unsettling, but we felt somehow detached from the consequences. American tourists and business travelers to other nations found that they had to pay more in dollars for hotel rooms and meals, but most Americans felt no immediate, direct impact from the fall of the dollar. The following graph illustrates the value of the dollar relative to an index of foreign currencies. Note particularly the decline of the dollar since 1985.

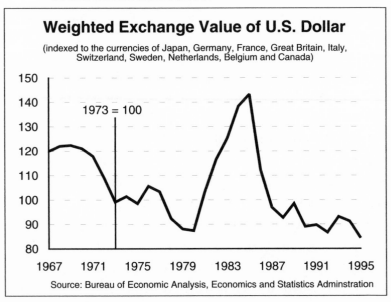

Weighted Exchange Value of U.S. Dollar

(indexed to the currencies of Japan, Germany, France, Great Britain, Italy, Switzerland, Sweden, Netherlands, Belgium and Canada)

1973 = 100

Source: Bureau of Economic Analysis, Economics and Statistics Adminstration

When the dollar moves significantly up or down, it is like dropping a large rock in a lake—the ripple effect is substantial. Too much fluctuation in the value of the dollar—in either direction—is not good for the economy of the United States or the world. The long-term trend is clear. The following graph shows the path of the dollar compared to the Japanese yen.

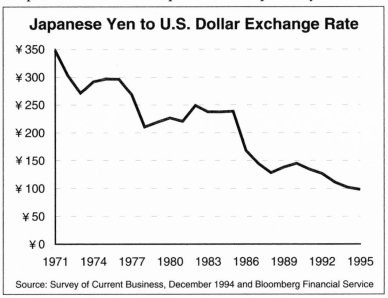

Japanese Yen to U.S. Dollar Exchange Rate

Source: Survey of Current Business, December 1994 and Bloomberg Financial Service

The relationship to the German mark is similar, though not as dramatic. For many years after World War II, the dollar was worth more than four marks. But by 1995, a dollar would buy only about 1.4 marks, as shown in the graph on the next page.

This downward trend should concern U.S. citizens and responsible people everywhere. A depreciating currency indicates a loss of confidence in that nation to provide economically stable leadership.

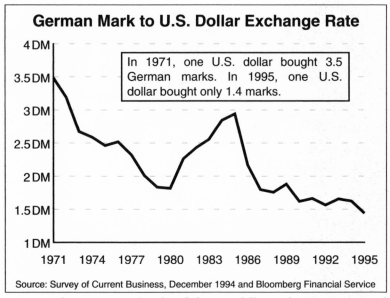

German Mark to U.S. Dollar Exchange Rate

In 1971, one U.S. dollar bought 3.5 German marks. In 1995, one U.S. dollar bought only 1.4 marks.

Source: Survey of Current Business, December 1994 and Bloomberg Financial Service

Almost two-thirds of the world's trade is transacted in dollars, but that percentage is slowly receding. Uncertainty about the dollar complicates world trade. Although approximately thirty-five nations still tie their currency directly to the value of the U.S. dollar, other countries now utilize a "market basket" concept that determines the value of their currency. This concept is similar to a mutual fund. The value of a nation's currency rises and falls depending on the values of the components contained in that nation's "portfolio," or market basket. The dollar is part of every market basket. Those market baskets also include the Japanese yen, the German mark, and other major currencies. In recent years, there has been slippage away from the dollar even in market basket nations. One such country, Norway, releases information about its currency (the kroner) to the public, but most nations do not. In 1982, Norway reduced the weight of the dollar in its market basket from 25 percent to 11 percent. This action is a clear indicator that Norway no longer had the confidence in the dollar that it once had.

While it is important to all nations that the United States maintains a stable currency, it is particularly important to the citizens of this country. For example, sales of crude oil are denominated in dollars even if no U.S. entity is involved in the transaction. If those sales were in yen or deutsche marks, and the downward trend in the dollar were to continue, the price of imported oil to the United States would escalate.

We use huge amounts of oil and oil-based products, such as gasoline and synthetics. If oil had been pegged to the yen in 1968, when a dollar bought 360 yen, we would be paying more than three times as much today for foreign oil and would suffer huge repercussions in our economy.

If the dollar continues to decline, oil-producing nations will eventually shift away from the dollar or include it in a market basket of currencies to arrive at a price for crude oil. Denominating the price of oil in a currency other than the dollar would place the United States in double jeopardy. We would be at risk of the oil-producing nations increasing the price they charge for their oil. Of course, we are already in that position today. But a potentially disastrous situation could result if, as described above, a new oil currency (say, deutsche marks) moved against the dollar in connection with an increase in the price of oil. If the dollar is no longer perceived as a strong, stable currency, there is nothing to prevent such a shift in oil pricing from happening.

The following graph indicates the extent to which the United States relies on foreign oil. After reaching a peak of almost 50 percent in 1977, our

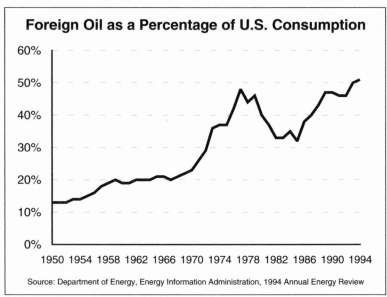

Foreign Oil as a Percentage of U.S. Consumption

Source: Department of Energy, Energy Information Administration, 1994 Annual Energy Review

consumption of foreign oil declined for the next few years. However, in 1985, the percentage of foreign oil consumed in the United States began to increase again. We now consume a greater percentage of foreign oil than we did during the oil shortage shocks of the 1970s.

Recent Events

What was the reaction to the declining value of the dollar in the spring of 1995, when it dropped below one hundred yen to the dollar? The British publication, *The Economist*, observed: "In the long run, the biggest loser from the neglect of the dollar will be America itself" (April 15, 1995).

When the value of the dollar dropped below eighty yen a few weeks later, what was the reaction of financial experts and commentators? A *Journal of Commerce* columnist accurately noted, "The weak dollar will decrease U.S. political influence abroad." Peter Passell wrote in *The New York Times* on May 7, 1995, **"No indicator of the American economic decline stands out like the fallen dollar."**

Two of the nation's most astute financiers offered some sobering thoughts about the situation. Paul Volcker, former chairman of the Federal Reserve Board, is quoted in *The New York Times* on May 2, 1995, as saying, "If you think American leadership

is important, then erosion [of the dollar] is a nega-
tive." In the March 20, 1995, issue of *Time*, Felix
Rohatyn said:

> *We are gradually losing control of our own des-*
> *tiny. The dollar's decline undercuts American*
> *economic leadership and prestige. It is perhaps*
> *the single most dangerous economic threat we*
> *will face in the long term because it puts us at*
> *the mercy of other countries.*

Should the situation need further elaboration, two
more articles looked at the situation from the per-
spective of our European and Asian trading partners. Van Ooms, an economist for the Committee
for Economic Development and former chief of
staff for the House Budget Committee, was quoted
in the pages of the *Chicago Tribune* on April 13,
1995, as saying that Europeans will take this country less seriously on foreign policy "when it can't
run a credible economic policy." As if to under-
score all of this, the April 12, 1995, edition of the
Wall Street Journal had a headline about the
fastest-growing economic part of the world. It was
headlined, "Asia's Central Banks Unloading Dollars
in Shift Toward Yen as Trade Currency." Once
again, confidence in the dollar is slipping.

After the dramatic decline of the dollar in April
1995, the central banks of other nations—their

equivalents of our Federal Reserve—moved to shore up the dollar, as did the U.S. Treasury and the Federal Reserve. They did this by purchasing Treasury securities of the U.S. government. A drop in the value of the dollar helps U.S. trade temporarily by making it easier for other nations to buy our products and harder for them to sell to us. That's the good news. The bad news is that a falling dollar is inflationary. Inflation causes the consumer dollar to shrink, thereby making everything more expensive. There is little incentive to save during an inflationary cycle because people would rather purchase goods and services at today's level, not after the prices have risen even more. To combat inflation, the Federal Reserve usually raises interest rates in an effort to dampen consumer borrowing and spending.

The result of the dollar's decline in 1995 can be seen by comparing two Federal Reserve reports. The first report, dated March 22, 1995, stated that central banks of other nations held $429 billion worth of U.S. bonds, called "Treasury securities" by financial people.

A report dated one year later, March 20, 1996, indicated that the holdings of these central banks had risen to $551 billion. The reason? In the spring of 1995, the central banks had bought our Treasury securities to bail out the dollar—that is, to lift the price of the dollar on the world markets.

The central banks of those foreign countries are under no obligation to hold the securities indefinitely. They will be particularly eager to sell them if it looks like the value of the dollar will dip once again. If there is such a decline, interest rates will have to rise to compensate the next owner of the securities for the additional amount of perceived risk to the capital. This will cause long-term harm to almost every aspect of our economy.

Higher interest rates discourage industrial investment because high rates diminish the profits from modernizing or building an industry. And when industries are not modernized, U.S. productivity declines. Higher interest rates hurt housing construction and sales. Purchases of new automobiles drop. In addition, we suffer a thousand and one other self-inflicted wounds affecting every American one way or another.

Foreign Holdings of U.S. Debt

The following graph shows that approximately 26 percent of the national debt—or about $1.3 trillion of the $5 trillion debt—is known to be held outside the United States.

The foreign holdings include the Treasury securities owned by foreign central banks as well as those owned by foreign individuals and foreign

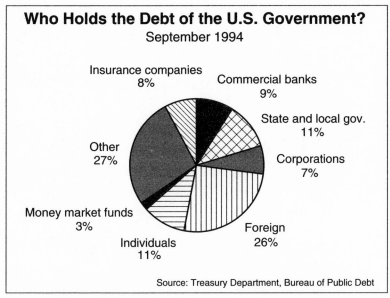

Who Holds the Debt of the U.S. Government?
September 1994

Insurance companies
8%

Commercial banks
9%

State and local gov.
11%

Other
27%

Corporations
7%

Money market funds
3%

Individuals
11%

Foreign
26%

Source: Treasury Department, Bureau of Public Debt

corporations. The national debt is represented by Treasury bills (maturity of less than one year), Treasury notes (maturity of one year to ten years), and Treasury bonds (maturity of ten years to thirty years) issued by the United States government.

Many foreign countries prohibit their residents from holding bonds issued by another nation. Earlier in our history, Americans also were not permitted to own bonds issued by other countries. As a result of the current prohibitions by other countries, additional actual foreign ownership remains undisclosed. The true ownership can be effectively concealed through a third party holding the securities. The following graph indicates the best estimate by the U.S. Treasury Department as to the regions of the world that held U.S. Treasury securities as of September 30, 1994.

Foreign Holdings of U.S. Treasury Securities
September 1994

International 1.7%

Europe 43.5%

Japan 27.4%

Australia 0.1%

Western Hemisphere 5.7%

Asia 20.5%

Africa 0.9%

Source: Treasury Department, Bureau of Public Debt

Less widely known is that 14 percent of the bonds issued by U.S.-based corporations are held by institutions and individuals beyond our borders. That money has financed much of our industrial expansion and modernization. Once again, if the dollar continues to decline, we will either lose this source of capital, or interest rates will have to rise to compensate investors. Neither result will help American workers employed by those companies.

Compounding the potential problem of our liabilities being held by foreign entities is the fact that our banks are holding a sizable amount of foreign assets in the form of savings and checking account deposits. Indirectly, those deposits help finance both the government sector and the private sector, because U.S. banks will use the foreign deposits to buy Treasury notes and to make loans to U.S. businesses. And, one more time, *if the depositors of this foreign money get nervous because of a fall in the dollar, the only way to salvage the situation will be with higher interest rates.*

In addition to the $1.3 trillion or more worth of U.S. Treasury securities under foreign ownership, there may be an additional $250 billion in U.S. currency held overseas. It is difficult to determine this amount with any degree of accuracy. This figure is the estimate of Lawrence Lindsey of the Federal Reserve Board. Unlike in the case with Treasury securities, the United States government pays no interest on these holdings. However, as with Treasury securities, the holders of U.S. currency can also become nervous about the value of the dollar. The problem in this situation, of course, is that a currency holder's only viable remedy is to sell dollars and buy another currency—for example yen or deutsche marks—with the proceeds. This would put even more pressure on the dollar. Although our government is not required to buy those dollars from foreign sellers, it may find itself in the position of having to do so in an effort to support the currency. Without going into a detailed explanation, the only mechanism available to the United States government for buying excess currency is to issue interest-bearing U.S. Treasury securities in exchange for the currency. The net result is that the interest-free deposits of U.S. currency previously held in foreign countries will be converted into additional interest-bearing debt of the federal government. A goal of the United States government should be less debt, not more debt.

The Almighty...Yen?

After the slide of the dollar in April 1995, the *Washington Post* published a column noting the opinion of two economic observers that the United States should consider issuing Treasury securities in yen rather than dollars. The reasoning is simple: Financial markets want a stable currency for their investments, particularly long-term investments. The purchaser of a twenty-year bond would like to be reasonably certain that the investment will not depreciate in value relative to other investments he or she might have made. The investor wants to count on the Treasury bond being worth ten thousand dollars at the end of twenty years. But if there is concern that the ten thousand dollars won't buy, say, a set of tires twenty years from now, then the investor is not likely to purchase U.S. bonds.

The yen has shown itself to be much more stable than the dollar. To continue to sell Treasury securities in dollars, the economists argue, will require higher interest rates than if the securities were denominated in yen. The idea is not new, and it will become an increasing possibility without currency stability. In 1978, on his last day as chairman of the Federal Reserve Board, Arthur Burns urged that at least ten billion dollars in Treasury securities be sold in other currencies.

But what looks good on paper to an economist looks like political dynamite to an office holder. If the United States moves in that direction, the move would be caused by severe economic necessity. Public opinion would strongly oppose it.

Economic Persuasion or Military Persuasion?

The United States is one of many nations in recent history that have gone through the struggle of watching their currencies decline. The British, under Prime Minister Harold Wilson, shook the financial world in 1967 when they devalued the pound sterling by 14 percent and increased their basic interest rate to 8 percent. Until that point, the world image of the British currency was that it was solid and favorable. But financial experts had known for many years before 1967 that the British were slipping economically.

Eleven years earlier, that slippage helped change history. In 1956, only eight days before the U.S. presidential election, the British, French, and Israelis invaded Egypt and seized the Suez Canal in response to hostile actions by Egypt's President Gamal Nasser. Because all three invading nations were our good friends, because President Eisenhower was in the midst of a reelection campaign, and because the invaders had misinterpreted conversations with U.S. Secretary of State John Foster Dulles, they felt safe in taking the military action without notifying the United States. To their surprise, President Eisenhower immediately denounced the invasion. He froze the assets of the British, French, Israelis, and Egyptians in the United States, and then our government quietly hinted at action that would harm the British pound sterling, already on shaky ground, if the troops were not withdrawn. The invasion ended without the United States firing a shot.

In more recent times, Saudi Arabia wanted to make an arms purchase from the United States that required congressional approval. The president asked Treasury Department officials to visit with members of the House and Senate who were hostile or wavering. The officials quietly explained that if the United States did not sell weapons to the Saudis, the Arab nation might stop buying U.S. securities that helped to finance our deficit and keep our dollar in relatively good shape.

As the preceding examples show, economic coercion can be as powerful as military coercion, or more so. Economic persuasion also has the advantage of being much less expensive and much more efficient than military operations.

In his book, *Day of Reckoning*, published in 1988, Benjamin Friedman of Harvard noted:

World power and influence have historically accrued to creditor nations. People simply do not regard their workers, their tenants and their debtors in the same light as their employers, their landlords and their creditors. Over time the respect, and even deference, that America had earned as world banker will gradually shift to the new creditor countries that are able to supply resources where we cannot, and America's influence over nations and events will ebb.

Another way of expressing the same thought more succinctly is with the widely accepted realization that a weak currency is the sign of a weak economy, and a weak economy leads to a weak nation.

Judged by military might, the United States is by far the most powerful nation in the world. Judged by economic standards, the United States is powerful but slipping. Strong economics alone do not make a strong nation, and a nation that is weakening on the economic front will play a diminished role in the community of nations.

More than two thousand years ago, King Solomon wrote in Proverbs: "The borrower is servant to the lender." So it will be unless the United States puts its economic house in order—and soon.

Chapter 4

What Is the Danger?

The first three chapters of this book present a quick history of coin and currency and a discussion of how the management, or mismanagement, of money can affect everyone. In this chapter, we look at the problems and dangers that past decisions hold for the people of today's world.

With the fall of the Soviet Union, what is the greatest danger facing the United States? Oddly enough, one of the biggest threats to our long-term security may be *perception*. If we are perceived as a first-rate military power but lacking the courage and common sense to handle our financial resources wisely, our influence will continue slowly waning. If we are unwilling to make even small sacrifices for our long-term good, other nations will doubt our commitment to help them with their long-term problems, whether economic or military. Today, our ability to stabilize the world economically and politically is being seriously questioned. **People and nations do not follow weak leaders. Sounding an uncertain trumpet on political and economic matters does not galvanize or inspire followers.**

Political Opportunities vs. Economic Realities

In his column for *The New York Times*, Thomas Friedman quoted Michael Mandelbaum, a foreign policy specialist with Johns Hopkins University, who said: "The French have the instincts of a traditional great power, but they don't have the means. The U.S. has the means, but it doesn't have the instincts." Unfortunately, there is much truth in that statement. The "instincts" referred to are the courage and commitment to do those things that must be done by a great nation. The reasons we have failed in this regard are both political and economic. The *political* reasons include:

- We lack courage and consistency on too many international fronts.
- We have failed to pay the more than $1.4 billion we owe the United Nations.
- We are dead last when compared with the Western European nations and Japan in the percentage of our national income that goes for foreign economic assistance.

- We have asked other nations to contribute troops to United Nations peacekeeping efforts, but we have contributed few ourselves. (Jordan and Nepal are ahead of us!)

The *economic* reasons can be boiled down to one phrase: failure to address our financial problems—particularly our budget deficit.

The collapse of the Soviet system raised our *political* fortunes and opportunities. Despite our weaknesses, we remain the world's most powerful military and political force, though declining in the latter. Our *economic* fortunes have gone up and down like the stock market, but the perception of weakness has caused the overall trend to be one of a sinking dollar, a weakening giant.

In both international and domestic politics, perception of strength adds to strength, and perception of weakness adds to weakness. To lead the world toward greater stability and away from the threats of war, the United States must show both political and economic strength.

Trading Places

Perhaps there is no other area where the political and economic fortunes of the United States are on display to the extent that they are in the field of international trade. In many ways, our recent history in foreign trade illustrates the problems and resulting dangers posed by a weakening dollar.

As discussed in greater detail in chapter 6, for most of this century the United States was the world's largest creditor nation. This simply means that we sold more goods and services to foreign countries than we purchased from them. As mentioned earlier, the United States changed from the largest creditor nation into the largest debtor nation practically overnight. We are buying more from foreign countries than we are selling to them. This drastic change is yet another component in the devaluation of the dollar.

There is no shortage of statistics on foreign trade. The two measurements most often quoted in the financial press are the *merchandise trade deficit* and the *current account balance*. The merchandise trade deficit measures the difference in the amount of tangible goods (clothes and televisions, for example) that we buy from foreign manufacturers versus the amount of tangible goods (airplanes, for example) that U.S. manufacturers sell to foreign countries. The United States has been running large merchandise trade deficits for the last nineteen years. The following graph indicates the extent to which our merchandise trade deficit has skyrocketed in the last few years.

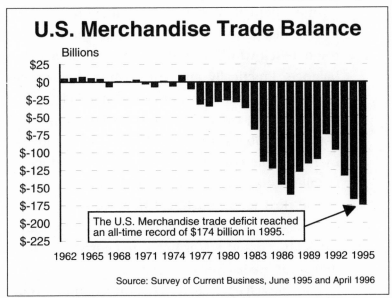

U.S. Merchandise Trade Balance

Billions

The U.S. Merchandise trade deficit reached an all-time record of $174 billion in 1995.

1962 1965 1968 1971 1974 1977 1980 1983 1986 1989 1992 1995

Source: Survey of Current Business, June 1995 and April 1996

The current account balance is a broader measure of commerce between the United States and other nations. The merchandise trade deficit is one component of the current account balance. The other components consist of:

- **Services:** such as engineering, legal, accounting, and management consulting.
- **Investment income:** the net difference between income earned by U.S. investors in foreign countries versus income earned by foreign investors in the United States.
- **Unilateral transfers:** primarily assistance by the U.S. government to foreign countries.

To the extent that these items can run a surplus instead of a deficit, they can offset the merchandise trade deficit when computing the current account balance. Practically speaking, while the services component always produces a surplus for the United States, the unilateral transfers component usually produces a deficit. And while the investment income component has usually produced a surplus, it has recently become a deficit.

The next table illustrates how we arrive at the current account balance. As the last column indicates, the United States has run a current account deficit for the last thirteen years.

The message is clear. The merchandise trade deficit overwhelms the other three components of the current account balance. The bottom line is that we are transferring our national wealth overseas. It should come as no surprise to us that foreign countries have the resources to purchase our Treasury securities—we have been financing those purchases with our current account deficit.

U.S. International Transactions
(millions of dollars)

	MERCHANDISE	SERVICES	INVESTMENT INCOME	UNILATERAL TRANSFERS	CURRENT ACCOUNT
	Net +	**Net** +	**Net** +	**Net** =	**Balance**
1970	2,603	(349)	6233	(6,156)	2,331
1971	(2,260)	957	7272	(7,402)	(1,433)
1972	(6,416)	973	8192	(8,544)	(5,795)
1973	911	989	12153	(6,913)	7,140
1974	(5,505)	1213	15503	(9,249)	1,962
1975	8,903	3501	12787	(7,075)	18,116
1976	(9,483)	3401	16063	(5,686)	4,295
1977	(31,091)	3845	18137	(5,226)	(14,335)
1978	(33,927)	4164	20408	(5,788)	(15,143)
1979	(27,568)	3003	30873	(6,593)	(285)
1980	(25,500)	6093	30073	(8,349)	2,317
1981	(28,023)	11852	32903	(11,702)	5,030
1982	(36,485)	12329	29788	(17,075)	(11,443)
1983	(67,102)	9335	31500	(17,718)	(43,985)
1984	(112,492)	3419	30720	(20,598)	(98,951)
1985	(122,173)	294	20590	(22,954)	(124,243)
1986	(145,081)	5530	12881	(24,189)	(150,859)
1987	(159,557)	6861	9465	(23,107)	(166,338)
1988	(126,959)	11635	13264	(25,023)	(127,083)
1989	(115,245)	23853	13659	(26,106)	(103,839)
1990	(109,030)	29037	20725	(33,393)	(92,661)
1991	(74,048)	44664	15111	6,869	(7,424)
1992	(96,106)	56626	10079	(32,148)	(61,549)
1993	(132,618)	57777	9000	(34,084)	(99,925)
1994	(166,099)	59887	(9,272)	(35,761)	(151,245)
1995	(174,469)	63050	(11,402)	(30,095)	(152,915)

Source: Survey of Current Business, June 1995, April 1996

Financing Our Deficit Abroad

The combination of trade deficits, the sale of our Treasury notes to cover our budget deficits, and the holding of the dollar in other countries for safety reasons has led to what economists call a *dollar overhang*. A dollar overhang occurs when the IOUs of the United States that we call dollars (both currency and securities) in the banks and pockets of people overseas are greater than our holdings of their currencies. In 1960, when dollars technically still could be exchanged for gold, people from other nations held $3 billion more in currency dollars than we held in gold reserves. In 1975, that "overhang" was somewhere between $100 and $150 billion, and today it is significantly larger. In *Day of Reckoning*, Harvard economist Benjamin Friedman describes the situation as "a flood of dollars that we have sent overseas to pay for our own trade imbalance."

The following choices are available to the foreign holder of dollars who is trying to decide what to do with them:

1. Hold on to dollars as a prized possession and as a safeguard against a local currency that might depreciate more than the dollar.
2. Convert the dollars into another currency, requiring Uncle Sam to "pay up" when the dollars are returned by the financial institution to the United States.

3. Use the dollars to buy real estate, stock, or some other chunk of America.
4. Use the dollars to buy consumer items that are still manufactured in America.

The third option has occurred with such frequency that the foreign ownership of farms, corporate stocks, and some other American enterprises has reached a mind-boggling level. Citizens of Great Britain, the Netherlands, Japan, and other nations have found U.S. real estate and businesses to be attractive assets. Foreign interests have built automobile plants in the United States, purchased Rockefeller Center, and sometimes simply put their money into savings accounts or certificates of deposit in our banks. But there has been a chill on such friendly acquisitions and deposits—a chill caused by the drop in the dollar and real estate prices.

The ability of the United States to finance the budget deficit, as well as industrial and real estate development, through foreign investment has diminished. But, no one is certain by how much. However, if the dollar declines and foreign investment continues, and unless we alter and improve our fiscal policies (primarily by balancing the budget), the answer we will be forced to accept is inevitable—higher interest rates will be necessary to attract the capital we need. For example, we sell approximately $200 billion a month in Treasury securities. If investors, both in the United States and abroad, believe that the dollars in which they will be repaid will be worth less in the future, they will require higher interest rates to compensate them for their risk—either real or imagined. Of course, higher interest rates discourage industrial investment and home construction, as well as causing many other troublesome consequences. The big losers when interest rates rise are the taxpayers of the United States.

In very simple terms, what it means is this: If interest rates on our Treasury securities increase only *one-tenth of 1 percent* and stay at that level for six years, taxpayers will pay an additional $20-$25 billion in interest on our federal debt. In his book *Zero-Sum Solution*, economist Lester Thurow concludes: "Foreign debts represent a direct one-for-one future (but no one knows when) reduction in American standards of living."

Consequences of Rising Interest Rates

Lack of stability in the international economic arena has been one of the reasons—but only one—for the number of U.S. savings and loan institutions failing in the last few decades. An example is a savings and loan that has a thirty-year mortgage on a home at 6 percent interest, a prevailing mortgage interest rate not too many years ago. But when inflation hit us, the savings and loans could not attract depositors at the low rate of return they were permitted to pay. They were then "freed" (through deregulation of the savings and loan industry) to *pay* higher interest rates, but were still *receiving* only 6 percent on their old mortgages. The squeeze put many of those institutions out of business very quickly.

The savings and loan owners who were able to survive for a while ventured into unfamiliar territory, looking in desperation for quick profits. While they may have understood residential lending, that knowledge did not successfully transfer to commercial lending in many cases. The results cost many of them their businesses, and cost the nation billions of dollars from our deposit insurance fund.

Commercial banks also suffered, but not as dramatically. Uncle Sam encouraged them to make loans in the international arena. As long as the dollar was stable, the risks were minimized. But, if a bank made a loan to a foreign corporation in dollars that were then converted into marks to be repaid at the same dollar-to-mark ratio in three years, and at the end of the three years the dollar has dropped 20 percent against the mark, the U.S. bank suffers a 20 percent loss. From 1968 to 1975, the mark grew 64 percent in value relative to the dollar. During a nine-month period beginning in 1985, the mark gained 22 percent against the dollar. In fluctuation periods like those, some of the larger banks suffered major losses .

Consequences of an Unstable Dollar

Stability of the dollar is important because a large increase or decrease in the value of the dollar causes turmoil in foreign economies, and that turmoil eventually hurts the United States. A shrinking dollar adds to inflation in the United States because foreign goods cost more. A round of inflation temporarily benefits manufacturers located in the United States because U.S.-made goods become cheaper to overseas buyers. However, the combination of a falling dollar and inflation can easily get out of control. As mentioned earlier, a drop in the dollar brings inflation, and inflation causes a greater drop in the dollar. Unless there is tough monetary medicine such as the high short-term interest rates that Federal Reserve Chairman Paul Volcker gave the nation in 1979—as well as changes in fiscal policy—the downward spiral will continue.

If a drop in the dollar is accompanied by widespread belief that the value will not fall much farther, foreign investors become willing and motivated to invest in the United States. That is both good news and bad news. The good news is that the

United States gets a new asset (BMW builds a plant in South Carolina, for example) and some U.S. dollars come back to this country in the process. The bad news is that we lose control of many of our assets (Rockefeller Center, though that has since been re-sold to U.S. interests at a loss to the Japanese purchasers). Part of the "dollar overhang" is used to buy our assets. A family that needs money can sell its car to pay debts, but few would say the family is richer as a result. The United States is like that family, selling our assets to pay our debts. Like a family, unless we break ourselves of the debt habit, we will eventually run out of assets to sell.

The results of a shifting dollar are not immediately apparent and seldom generate an outcry from the citizens, but political leaders know that repercussions will usually follow. Hobart Rowen, economic writer of the *Washington Post*, asserted that President Lyndon Johnson's "sudden decision to neither seek nor accept the nomination of his party" was triggered as much by "loss of [international] confidence in the dollar as by public opposition to the [Vietnam] war—though this was barely recognized at the time." Adding some credibility to Rowen's assertion is that two weeks before the president's stunning announcement, the results of an eight-nation meeting on gold and the dollar clearly spelled trouble for the future of the dollar.

The great danger from an unstable dollar is that it creates uncertainty in international economics. The world's economy, including the economy of the United States, grew at a remarkable rate for more than two decades after World War II, thanks in large part to the Bretton Woods agreement that gave the world a stable dollar as the basis for international trade. The next graph shows the growing world economy. Industrial investments that improve productivity and raise standards of living are less likely to be made in the atmosphere of an uncertain currency. Some transactions have been shifted to the Japanese yen and the German mark, but neither represents the economic clout of the United States and the dollar. "Market baskets" of

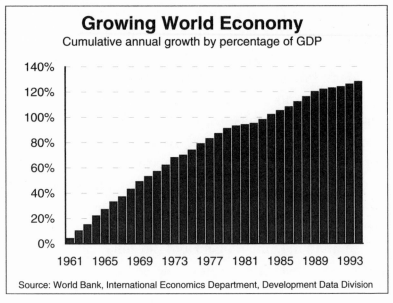

Growing World Economy

Cumulative annual growth by percentage of GDP

Source: World Bank, International Economics Department, Development Data Division

currencies offer protection, but they are complicated to administer in transactions between nations.

Advantages of a Stable Currency

If the European nations can agree on a solid plan for a common currency, and should they also agree that all members will sacrifice to back that currency if necessary, the dollar might be displaced in world trade. This process would take time, and it would take cooperation among the European powers—cooperation that is now much greater than in the pre-World War II period, but not yet good enough to create a world-class currency.

The latest effort is to create a single European currency by January 1, 1999. If created, it will be called the *euro*. To become a member nation of the currency block, each country must meet certain standards as evidence of its ability to support the value of the euro. If the United States were located in Europe and eligible for membership in the European Community, could it meet the standards? Probably not! Two requirements in particular would pose problems for the United States.

First, a nation's budget deficit cannot exceed 3 percent of its gross domestic product. For the fiscal year ending September 30, 1995, the gross domestic product of the United States was $7 trillion. Three percent of that amount is equal to $210 billion. The federal budget deficit for fiscal year 1995 was $164 billion, so the United States would have met the first requirement. However, we would have failed this test for the fiscal year ending in 1994. The following graph shows how the U.S. would have fared in this financial requirement since 1940.

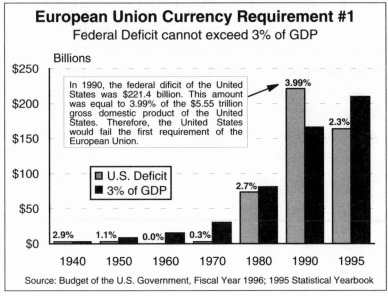

European Union Currency Requirement #1
Federal Deficit cannot exceed 3% of GDP

In 1990, the federal dificit of the United States was $221.4 billion. This amount was equal to 3.99% of the $5.55 trillion gross domestic product of the United States. Therefore, the United States would fail the first requirement of the European Union.

■ U.S. Deficit
■ 3% of GDP

Source: Budget of the U.S. Government, Fiscal Year 1996; 1995 Statistical Yearbook

The second requirement could not be met now nor anytime in the near future. This standard provides that a nation's accumulated indebtedness cannot exceed 60 percent of its gross domestic product. Sixty percent of the $7 trillion figure mentioned above is $4.2 trillion, and the debt of the United States crossed the $5 trillion mark early in 1996. The next graph displays the second European Union financial requirement for the United States.

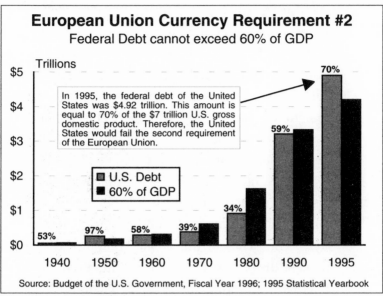

European Union Currency Requirement #2
Federal Debt cannot exceed 60% of GDP

Trillions

In 1995, the federal debt of the United States was $4.92 trillion. This amount is equal to 70% of the $7 trillion U.S. gross domestic product. Therefore, the United States would fail the second requirement of the European Union.

☐ U.S. Debt
■ 60% of GDP

Source: Budget of the U.S. Government, Fiscal Year 1996; 1995 Statistical Yearbook

In other words, if the United States were located in Europe, we would not be permitted to join in a European currency because we have followed policies that have weakened us too much.

Why is Europe moving in the direction of a common currency? There are basically three reasons:

- It further reduces the likelihood of European nations fighting each other, because of their increased cooperation and economic interdependence.
- It reduces trade barriers among the nations while strengthening their economies.
- **There is concern that the strength of the dollar is declining.**

This third reason is of major concern. If the dollar continues to fall, and if the European nations fail in their currency effort, world commerce will continue to grow, but not to its full potential. If the United States will face its problems and stabilize the dollar, there can be significant growth in world trade. The economies of the United States and many other countries will thrive and prosper. A rising tide truly can lift all boats.

If we flounder, and the dollar remains an uncertain basis for trade, our nation will suffer along with the community of nations. As Yale historian Diane Kunz says, "The death of the dollar order will drastically increase the price of the American dream while simultaneously shattering American global influence."

In an essay written seventy years ago, economist John Maynard Keynes said, "There is no subtler nor surer means of overturning the existing basis of society than to debauch the currency." When the value of a currency declines dramatically, the form of government accepted by the people of that nation often goes down with it.

Ignoring our budget problems will only result in higher debt and a lower value of the dollar. As time passes with no resolution to the crisis, the temptation of political leaders will be to tolerate greater and greater inflation. In this scenario, there is only one result—a lower standard of living for our people. **Political chaos may then follow. That is the lesson of history—that is the danger.**

Part Two

How Do We Solve It?

"The budget should be balanced.

"The treasury should be refilled. Public debt should be reduced.

"The arrogance of the public officials should be controlled."

CICERO
106-43 B.C.

Chapter 5

Balance the Budget

The first four chapters of this book diagnose the illnesses afflicting the U.S. dollar and clearly outline the danger that will face us if we do not do something—and do it immediately. What is needed now is a prescription for those ailments. The next five chapters provide a blueprint for the steps that must be taken to solve our problems and to return the country and its people to the position of economic and political leadership formerly held for decades.

In seeking solutions, we must recognize that it is no mere coincidence that as the deficits of the federal government have grown out of control during the last thirty years, the value of the dollar has declined. Since 1965, we have run a budget deficit every year except one—1969—as shown in the graph on the next page.

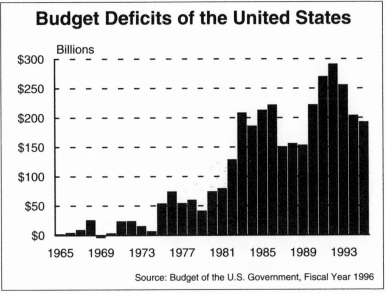

Budget Deficits of the United States

Billions

Source: Budget of the U.S. Government, Fiscal Year 1996

Four economists, looking at all the world's currencies in a study for the International Monetary Fund, concluded, "A sustained reduction in the government budget deficit that raises national saving and reduces the ratio of government debt to GDP (national income) will eventually lead to a real exchange rate appreciation." Putting it more bluntly, they say that decreasing government debt increases the value of the currency.

There are those who view the fall of the dollar as an event similar to an earthquake—no one can do anything to prevent it. After the decline of the dollar in the spring of 1995, the *Washington Post* editorialized:

Anger and frustration in their voices, Japanese

and German officials have been calling on the United States to do something about the [falling] dollar…The United States is likely to offer sympathy but little more. There's nothing useful that the United States can do.

Contrary to the analysis expressed in the *Post*, there *are* viable alternatives available to halt the slide of the dollar. On the one hand, our government can take actions that shore up the dollar *temporarily* in the vain hope that those actions will somehow produce a lasting benefit—or at least soften political and editorial criticism. Raising interest rates is a quick, but short-term option. So long as there is confidence that our currency will not depreciate too much, the high interest rate "cure" will provide temporary relief. However, high interest rates combined with a high dollar can produce harmful effects, such as unemployment. For example, during the 1970s unemployment was 6.2 percent. By 1980, the unemployment rate was 7.1 percent, and by 1982 the unemployment rate had peaked at 9.7 percent. We had that unhappy combination in the early 1980s. That solution also brings long-term problems, including larger trade deficits, bigger federal government deficits, and less industrial investment.

On the other hand, a more viable solution for halting the slide of the dollar is to increase the savings rate within the United States. This would certainly provide long-term help. And if there is confidence in the procedures used to increase the savings rate, it also would probably bring about short-term relief from a sliding dollar. Few sensible people would disagree with economist Martin Feldstein that, "The long-run pursuit of sound monetary and fiscal policies is the best way to avoid substantial swings in the dollar's value." Monetary policy in the United States, under the leadership of Federal Reserve Board Chairmen Paul Volcker and Alan Greenspan in recent years, has been essentially sound. Our problem has been fiscal policy.

One course of fiscal action will help both the short-term and the long-term outlook for the dollar—eliminating the budget deficit of the federal government as soon as possible. This option for halting the fall of the dollar—balancing the federal budget—is supported by convincing empirical evidence.

The Balanced Budget Amendment

The passage of the Balanced Budget Amendment to the Constitution in the House of Representatives and its subsequent defeat by one vote in the Senate provided a great deal of congressional drama during 1995. Let's take a brief look at the major provisions of this proposed constitutional Balanced Budget Amendment. The amendment:

- Directs the president to submit a balanced budget.
- Prohibits total outlays from exceeding total receipts for a fiscal year, unless three-fifths of the members of each house of Congress provide by law for a specific excess of outlays over receipts by a roll-call vote.
- Sets a permanent limit on the amount of the public debt and prohibits an increase in such amount unless approved by a three-fifths majority in each house by roll-call vote.
- Prohibits a bill to increase revenue from becoming law unless approved by a majority in each house by roll-call vote.
- Waives the provisions of this amendment for any fiscal year in which a declaration of war is in effect, or if the United States faces an imminent and serious military threat to national security as declared by a joint resolution which becomes law.

The sudden plunge in the dollar during the spring of 1995 occurred the day after the Senate failed by one vote to pass the Balanced Budget Amendment to the Constitution. Investors around the world lost confidence in the dollar because they perceived that our government was not serious about solving its fiscal problems.

An article appearing in the *Los Angeles Times* summarized an interview with Alan Greenspan, chairman of the Federal Reserve Board, shortly after that fateful vote was cast:

> *Last week's Senate defeat of the Balanced Budget Amendment [can be blamed] for the sudden plunge in the value of the dollar and he pointedly warned Congress that the currency will remain under long-term pressure until Washington tackles the deficit.*

The article noted that Mr. Greenspan's comments were "extraordinary because he so rarely gets involved in political disputes over tax and budget policies." A month later, *The New York Times* reported: "The Germans and the Japanese say the basic problem is America's budget deficit." *Business Week*, commenting on what it called "that sense of unease [caused by] the narrow defeat in the Senate of the Balanced Budget Amendment," noted the following:

> *What the [international] market wants is simple: less debt or higher interest... Investors are worrying that talk of tax cuts will continue despite the [balanced budget]*

amendment's failure. The optimism that something would be done on the long-standing U.S. budget deficit problem has disappeared, argues Jonathon H. Francis, head of Boston's Putnam Investments.

During the same period, Paul McCracken, a noted economist at the University of Michigan and former chair of the Council of Economic Advisers under President Nixon, wrote a guest column in the *Wall Street Journal* under the headline, "Falling Dollar? Blame the Deficit." The headline leaves little doubt as to McCracken's conclusion about the cause of the declining dollar.

The flip side of the empirical evidence occurred two months later, when it became clear that Congress was serious about balancing the budget and taking some tough steps to get there. The dollar rose in value. Even action by the Senate Budget Committee alone toward balancing the budget had a positive impact. The headline of an article in *The New York Times* on May 12, 1995, read, "The Dollar Surges On New Plan To Cut Deficit." The article, written by Peter Truell, begins, "The dollar staged its biggest one-day rally in nearly *four years*, rebounding against the German mark and the Japanese yen on *speculation* that Washington might do more than in the past to cut the federal budget deficit" [italics added]. The central banks of Germany and Japan, as well as our Federal Reserve, helped the rebound, but no one questions that congressional action on the deficit was the primary cause for the decline and then the rise in the dollar.

Although the 1996 budget battle will be remembered for the three government shutdowns, some positive steps did occur. Under the leadership of Sen. Pete Domenici, R-New Mexico, and Rep. John Kasich, R-Ohio, the first balanced budget plan submitted by Congress helped the dollar to rebound. Before the adoption of the 1996 budget, Trudy Rubin wrote in the *Journal of Commerce*, "If there were signs that Washington were cutting the deficit, the dollar would probably stabilize." She turned out to be correct. Lawrence Thimerene, chief economist for the Economic Strategy Institute, wrote in *The New York Times* that to stabilize the dollar, Congress and the president must "demonstrate real seriousness on deficit reduction."

To his credit, President Bill Clinton took steps to lower the deficit in 1993. His budget consisted of tax increases and spending cuts. While the authors have differing opinions about the use of an income tax increase to reduce the deficit, both authors agree with the concept of reducing the growth rate of the federal government. And to their credit, under the leadership of Senator Domenici and Representative Kasich, the Republicans in Congress introduced a seven-year plan to balance the budget.

The difficulty with the legislative approach to balancing the budget is that it has been tried before and does some good for about two years, but then it is abandoned. If the legislative approach were fortified by a constitutional amendment, the chances of actually achieving a balanced budget would be much greater. The financial markets of the world would react with lower interest rates and a firm position for the dollar as the world's premier currency.

No Pain, No Gain

Using the legislative approach alone is like a New Year's resolution to diet. Even if the diet is followed for only a short time, it's better than nothing. But the record for successful New Year's resolutions is disappointing. This fiscal diet has started with a great big dessert called a tax break: not a good way to start any meaningful diet. Most of the really tough decisions are reserved for the latter part of the seven years, when balance is supposed to be achieved.

This is like a New Year's resolution to lose fifty pounds. Assume that a friend of yours sets a goal of three pounds a month for the first ten months and ten pounds each for November and December. The plan is flawed from inception, because the odds are high that the holiday season will be too tempting once it arrives. Tomorrow never comes for the dieter or the budgeteer when the heavy lifting is deferred beyond a reasonable horizon.

In 1985, Congress passed the Gramm-Rudman-Hollings bill, named for Sens. Phil Gramm, R-Texas, Warren Rudman, R-New Hampshire, and Fritz Hollings, D-South Carolina. It called for balancing the budget in six years, and it did result in restrained spending for about two years. But in the fiscal year scheduled to balance the budget, the deficit reached $269 billion. It surely would have been worse without Gramm-Rudman-Hollings, but the measure's impact turned out to be limited.

The failure of the Gramm-Rudman-Hollings budget-balancing law to control deficit spending indicates the need for an amendment to the Constitution providing that the budget will be balanced each year. A constitutional amendment is our only reasonable hope for preventing lawmakers from spending beyond our means.

Economist Alan Blinder, a soon-to-retire member of the Federal Reserve Board, described the situation in 1985 when the nation found itself with a $200 billion budget deficit and a $150 billion trade deficit:

> *Everyone seemed to agree that the budget deficit was too big. Economists insisted that shrinking the budget deficit was the key to shrinking the foreign trade deficit. Both outcomes were devoutly desired. With this much national consensus, you might expect decisive action. Instead, we got paralysis as politicians argued over why the deficit was so large and how it should be cut.*

Without a constitutional balanced-budget amendment, such a stalemate probably will be repeated in the years ahead. There are no popular ways to cut deficits, and politicians like to do popular things.

No matter how much resolve Congress can temporarily muster, the long-term solution to the chronic deficit situation remains the constitutional amendment. It is not a new solution to the chronic deficit situation. While Thomas Jefferson was in Paris negotiating for our new government in 1787, James Madison and others were writing the Constitution. After Jefferson returned, he said that if he could add one amendment to the Constitution, it would be to prohibit the federal government from borrowing money. He wrote, "We should consider ourselves unauthorized to saddle posterity with our debts, and morally bound to pay them ourselves."

The constitutional amendment that the House passed and the Senate defeated by only one vote in 1995 did not absolutely prohibit the federal government from borrowing money, as Jefferson suggested. The authors of this book believe there are rare occasions, such as a war or a recession, when the federal government may need to spend more than its revenue. But government spending should not exceed revenue for twenty-seven consecutive years, as we have done.

Maybe Economists Can Agree

As demonstrated immediately above, finer minds than the authors' have already addressed the problem of government debt. Let's see what others have had to say about the problems associated with chronic deficit spending.

One of the nation's leading economists, Fred Bergsten, director of the Institute for International Economics, strongly supports a balanced-budget constitutional amendment. He believes that, in light of the need for an occasional stimulus when the economy dips, we should not "move to balance but try to move to a modest surplus as the steady state, and then in recession periods you can move back to balance and get some net stimulus to the economy."

In light of the changes that we know occur in the world from year to year, this is a very practical approach. It makes sense that a country as sophisticated as the United States should anticipate that extraordinary expenditures for natural disasters such as hurricanes, earthquakes, and floods will be required from time to time. It also makes sense, therefore, that to have the necessary resources available, a surplus must be created in the normal times. Therefore, the steady state of the U.S. budget should not be a deficit or even balance, but a small surplus.

Think of it in these terms. At home with our families, we are always trying to save for a rainy day. Why should it be different for our country? No prudent family plans to spend more than it brings home, and no prudent family plans to spend every penny in an effort to "break even." When possible, families try to save as they go. So, too, should our government.

This constitutional amendment, with strong bipartisan support, says that the budget must be balanced unless Congress approves deficit spending by a 60 percent majority, a margin that is not easy to achieve. That makes it difficult, but not impossible, to run an occasional deficit. That is the way it should be.

For fiscal year 1997, it is estimated that the *net* interest expenditure of the federal government will be $241 billion. The authors remember fiscal year

1962, when the *total budget* of the federal government topped $100 billion for the first time. The $257 billion for net interest is *nine times* more than the federal government will spend on education, *eleven times* as much as we will spend on our natural resources and environment, and *fifteen times* more than we will spend on foreign economic assistance. (What many consider a more accurate gauge, *gross* interest, will be $344 billion—even worse.) Paying excessive interest is simply a foolish way to spend money. The following graph shows the percentage of the U.S. budget devoted to paying *net* interest on the debt relative to other government expenditures.

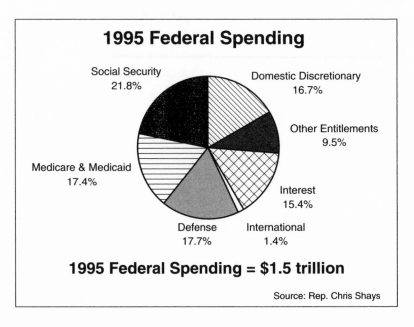

1995 Federal Spending

- Social Security 21.8%
- Domestic Discretionary 16.7%
- Other Entitlements 9.5%
- Medicare & Medicaid 17.4%
- Interest 15.4%
- Defense 17.7%
- International 1.4%

1995 Federal Spending = $1.5 trillion

Source: Rep. Chris Shays

The next graph shows the amount of the annual interest payments since 1965.

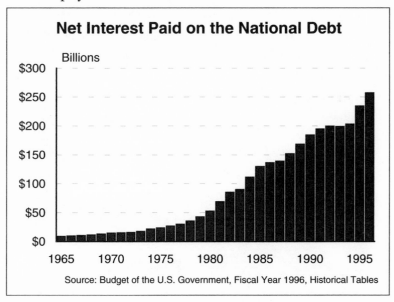

Net Interest Paid on the National Debt

Source: Budget of the U.S. Government, Fiscal Year 1996, Historical Tables

In 1988, economist Benjamin Friedman wrote:

The chronic federal deficit is sapping our productivity at home and our ability to compete abroad. As a result, our standard of living has already begun to grow more slowly, and America's influence in world affairs has suffered. If we do nothing to correct the problem, both our standard of living and our global power will continue to weaken. Ultimately, the resulting decay will threaten our society's most fundamental values.

When Dr. Friedman wrote that passage, our federal debt was $2.6 trillion, and seven years later, as this book goes to press, the figure exceeds $5 trillion.

Former Sen. Paul Tsongas, D-Massachusetts, testifying before a Senate Committee considering the constitutional amendment to balance the budget, stated:

If you ask yourself why are these deficits always voted for, the answer is very simple… there are a lot of votes in deficit spending. There are no votes in fiscal discipline. What you have here is a sad case of pursuit of self as opposed to pursuit of what is in the national interest. The balanced budget amendment is simply a recognition of that human behavior.

The evidence is overpowering that we are harming ourselves and that Thomas Jefferson was correct about not borrowing money. In addition to the distortions in federal spending caused by huge interest payments, a constitutional amendment to impose discipline where none currently exists is needed to protect the future of our nation.

In his classic book, *The Wealth of Nations*, published in 1776, Adam Smith observed that historically nations accumulate more and more debt, and then, in one way or another, they renounce their debt. He wrote:

> *When national debts have once been accumulated to a certain degree, there is scarce, I believe, a single instance of their having been fairly and completely paid. The liberation of the public revenue...has always been brought about by a bankruptcy...The raising of the denomination of the coin has been disguised...The creditors of the public are really defrauded. Almost all states... ancient as well as modern, when reduced to this necessity have...played this very juggling trick.*

Without constitutional restraint, we are headed in the same direction.

There are only three ways for a nation to pay its debt:

- Spend less.
- Tax more.
- Print more money.

The most politically attractive of these three alternatives, unfortunately, is printing more money. It is also the most dangerous of the three, because it puts too much money into circulation.

Stop the Presses!

While there is a temporary dip in the size of the deficit as a result of the Clinton administration's spending cuts and tax increases in 1993, and the Republican budget actions of 1995, there is a strong probability that we will soon see deficits climb to a level far beyond anything we have known. Until we confront the looming problem posed by the imminent crisis in Medicare financing and the aging of the baby boomers, we are ignoring the reality of the situation.

This level of deficit spending will go far beyond the point that nations tolerate before they begin a process economists refer to as "monetizing the debt." Economists usually try to explain this process by noting that it involves the printing of money to pay the debt. Strictly speaking, the government would not actually roll the printing presses and churn out new paper currency to pay off the debt to any great extent. That happened in a different era. It would actually be done with electronic debits and credits between financial institutions. But, the bottom line is the same— technically, the debt could get paid, but it would be at the expense of creating dollars that are worth far less because of runaway inflation.

One of the more important jobs of the Federal Reserve Board is to determine the proper level of money that is available. We usually hear about this activity in terms of something called the "money supply." If there is too much money in circulation, prices go up, which means the dollar is worth less. Economists usually refer to this situation as "too many dollars chasing too few goods." Then wages have to increase so that everyone can buy the more expensive merchandise. The Federal Reserve Board spends much of its time keeping inflation under control.

For many reasons, the authors do not advocate returning to the gold standard. But we recognize that in the past it had the advantage of securing our currency to a solid base, and it limited our ability to create debt. It is interesting to note that for the twenty years before the United States went off the gold standard, inflation averaged 2.3 percent per year. For the twenty years after we abandoned the gold standard, inflation averaged 6.3 percent per year. The graph on the next page illustrates the point.

While paying debt the easy way—just printing more money—may sound attractive, the depreciation of the dollar will mean great harm to family savings and pension plans. That is why the chief actuary of the Social Security Administration for twenty-one years, Robert Myers, says that it is essential for the future of Social Security that we have

Inflation Before and After 1971

Inflation Rate

U.S. Dollar taken off gold standard

14%
12%
10%
8%
6%
4%
2%
0%
-2%

1951 1955 1959 1963 1967 1971 1975 1979 1983 1987 1991

Source: Dept. of Labor, Bureau of Labor Statistics, Division of Foreign Labor Statistics

a balanced-budget amendment to the Constitution. If, for example, by printing more money, the dollar is made worth only one-tenth of its current value, the Social Security trust funds are also made worth only one-tenth of their current value—at the very time that retirees need more money to sustain themselves. In other words, if the government uses the crutch of printing more money to "solve" its problem, a family that has saved for forty years would soon realize that it cannot afford to retire. If it had saved $100,000, it would only have the spending power of one-tenth that amount, or ten thousand dollars. Can you imagine the public outcry if this were to come to pass?

Don't take our word for what may happen. Look at the following chart, prepared for fiscal year 1995 by the Clinton administration's Office of Management and Budget.

Lifetime Net Tax Rates Under Alternative Policies		
Birth Year	Before Clinton	After Clinton
1900	23.6	23.6
1910	27.2	27.2
1920	29.0	29.1
1930	30.5	30.6
1940	31.6	31.9
1950	32.8	33.2
1960	34.4	35.0
1970	35.7	36.5
1980	36.0	36.9
1990	35.5	36.5
Future Generations	93.7	82.0

The "Before" and "After" columns refer to the time periods before and after President Clinton's 1993 effort to reduce the deficit.

If you were born in 1930, your lifetime net tax bill will be about 30 percent of your income. But go down to our future citizens. For someone born in 1995, according to this estimate, taxes will consume 82 percent of lifetime income. That won't happen. Political realities will not let it happen, or we will see another American Revolution. Before that occurs, the nation will roll the printing presses to "print ourselves out of this problem," creating many of the inflationary problems that were previously discussed. A much wiser course of action is to get the deficit under control now and not bring on the kind of political chaos that will occur long before we get close to an 82 percent tax rate.

Pay-as-You-Go Is the Way to Go

The biggest public works project in the history of humanity is the U.S. Interstate Highway system. To his great credit, President Eisenhower proposed it. But he also recommended that the project be financed by the sale of bonds. A senator from Tennessee, Albert Gore Sr. (father of the vice president in the Clinton administration), said that would be foolish. He proposed raising the gasoline tax and building the system on a pay-as-you-go basis. Fortunately, Sen. Gore's logic prevailed, saving the nation hundreds of billions of dollars in interest payments.

The bipartisan watchdog organization, Concord Coalition, has analyzed the deficit to determine what it has cost us over the last two decades. **The study concluded that income would be $15,500 per family higher each year if we had balanced our budget over the last two decades.**

Speaking of balancing the budget, what if a constitutional amendment had been in place in 1980 when the national debt totaled less than $1 trillion?

Instead of paying $344 billion in gross interest during fiscal year 1996, we would pay less than $70 billion. Actually, the bill would be appreciably less than this amount because interest rates would be much lower. Even after World War II, with the inflationary pressures of that period, the prime rate of interest was only 2.03 percent in 1946. A constitutional restriction would have given us more than $300 billion extra today for education or health care or reducing taxes. Because lower interest rates would have encouraged more industrial investment and home building, our productivity and standard of living would be much higher than they are today.

The preceding paragraph was, of course, a huge "what if." Let's look at the real world today. President Gerald Ford put it well when he said:

Unless we as a nation face up to the facts of fiscal reality and responsibility, and the sacrifices required to restore it, the economic time bomb we are sitting on will do us in as surely as any sudden enemy assault. We cannot go on living beyond our means by borrowing from future generations or being bailed out by foreign investors.

All of these admonitions for a sound fiscal policy are based on the assumption that we will also have a sound monetary policy from the Federal Reserve Board. While mistakes in judgment undoubtedly have been made from time to time by the Federal Reserve Board, the primary source of our difficulty since World War II has been fiscal policy, not monetary policy. **We need a pay-as-you-go government.**

Because the United States represents such a significant portion of the world's economy, interest rates around the world rise when we are forced to borrow to finance our deficit spending. Higher interest rates mean that people pay more for home mortgages than they should, more for cars, and more for anything purchased on credit.

Higher interest rates also mean that poor nations must pay more for interest because wealthy Uncle Sam does not have the good sense to put our government on a pay-as-you-go basis. In describing the economic problems of developing nations, Johns Hopkins University international specialist David Calleo wrote:

> *Above all, they blamed American fiscal policy, whose deficit financing would apparently require a large part of the world's available savings for the foreseeable future. To many it seemed highly unnatural, not to say obscene, that the world's richest country should also be its biggest borrower.*

All of these writers and commentators are speaking with common sense. **They are essentially saying that each generation must have the courage and discipline to pay its own way.** Failure to do so is no less insidious than borrowing a dollar from your ten-year old daughter and refusing to pay it back.

Who Should Do the Paying as We Go?

Achieving a balanced budget will not be easy. We have plenty of evidence on that point, but the authors believe that a constitutional amendment is required to reach that goal. All forms of revenue and expenditures should be on the table—entitlements, taxes, defense, and all the social programs. Everything. That includes something called "indexing," whereby the spending in certain federal programs is increased to compensate for the inflation rate. More and more of our federal expenditures are indexed, and as economists Arthur Burns and Paul Volcker have warned, indexing adds to inflation. But indexing is politically popular. More accurate calculation of indexing would save big money and help the economy.

The Advisory Commission to study the Consumer Price Index (the way we measure inflation) reported to Sen. William Roth, R-Delaware, and Sen. Daniel Patrick Moynihan, D-New York, in 1995 that inflation is probably overestimated between 0.7 percent and 2 percent, probably closer to 2 percent. For example, the Consumer Price Index (CPI) deals with a fixed market basket each month, assuming Americans buy certain items. But it does not permit flexibility. If the price of beef goes up, many people switch to chicken, but that is not taken into account. That is one small example. The commission worded it this way: "Consumers respond to price changes by moving away from products that have become more expensive and toward goods whose prices have declined."

If, in fact, the CPI overestimates inflation, then the federal government could save a great deal of money by making minor adjustments. If the CPI were reduced by 0.5 percent—less than the commission believes is desirable—in the year 2005, the savings would be $73 billion. If a figure of 1 percent were used, the savings would be approximately $140 billion in just one fiscal year.

Some politicians view indexing as a sacred cow, but they shouldn't. Everything must be on the table if we are truly serious about balancing the budget.

If we undertake balancing the budget as a top priority, and all of us sacrifice a little, everyone will benefit. A General Accounting Office study shows that if we balance the budget and stick with it, by the year 2020 the average American will have an inflation-adjusted increase in income of 36 percent. Otherwise, as we saw in the chart on page 87, which looked at the Lifetime Net Tax Rates, the result will be devastating to the country and to its citizens.

Economist Benjamin Friedman concluded his book *Day of Reckoning* with these words:

> *Adopting a different fiscal policy is not just an economic desideratum but a moral imperative. If we do not correct America's fiscal course, our children and our children's children will have the right to hold us responsible. The saddest outcome of all would be for America's decline to go on, but to go on so gradually that by the time the members of the next generation are old enough to begin asking who was responsible for their diminished circumstances, they will not even know what they have lost.*

Instead of living on a huge credit card and giving our children and grandchildren more debt and a lower standard of living, we can give our children and future generations a significantly improved standard of living.

That's worth fighting for!

Chapter 6

Reduce the Trade Deficit

T hroughout this book, the primary focus has been on the budget deficit of the United States government as the primary culprit for the falling dollar. It has been noted that the budget deficit for the fiscal year ending September 30, 1995, was $164 billion, and that the total national debt on that date stood at approximately $4.9 trillion. Unfortunately, the budget deficit is not the only deficit in town.

Exporting Our Wealth

Although the trade deficit, like the budget deficit, is a measure of revenues and expenditures, the trade deficit is not completely subject to the control of the government as is the budget deficit. However, many factors that ultimately determine the size of the trade deficit are heavily influenced by government action. For example, tariff policies directly affect the level of trade between our country and our foreign trading partners. Also, the government has the authority to restrict the private sector from trading with certain countries.

The most influential factor in the trade deficit is our old friend from previous chapters—the value of the dollar. The value of the dollar determines how much an overseas buyer can purchase from a U.S. company. Conversely, it also determines how much a U.S. buyer can afford to pay for a foreign product. The U.S. trade deficit for calendar year 1995 was $174 billion. Simply put, in 1995 we bought more from other nations than they bought from us, by a huge margin. The following graph shows the difference between our merchandise imports and exports over the last twenty-one years.

U.S. Merchandise Trade Comparison

Billions

Source: Survey of Current Business, June 1995 and April 1996

It is probably no coincidence that the beginning of the period of sustained trade deficits began in 1975—the same year that the budget deficits increased nine times to a then-record high of $53 billion.

On December 31, 1994, the accumulated trade deficit of the previous two years totaled approximately $1.1 trillion. This number is analogous to our national debt of $4.9 trillion. Like the national debt, the accumulated trade deficit will have to be paid, either by a lower standard of living or increased productivity and sales.

For most of this century, the United States sold more to other nations than they bought from us. However, we began to reverse field in a major way in 1976. The previous year, 1975, was the last year the United States posted a merchandise trade surplus. We moved from the No. 1 spot in world trade balance to dead last. It's like being the Super Bowl champion for many years and then suddenly having the worst record, by far, of any team.

What can we do about it? There is no single "silver bullet" that can solve this problem. The answers are complex. For example, the conventional wisdom says that a drop in the value of the dollar encourages exports and discourages imports. Over time, that is true.

However, from 1982 to 1994, the dollar dropped significantly in value—more than half compared to the yen—while our imports grew three times faster in those years than our purchase of domestic goods. The following graph shows this trend.

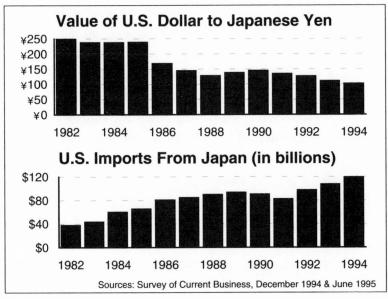

Value of U.S. Dollar to Japanese Yen

U.S. Imports From Japan (in billions)

Sources: Survey of Current Business, December 1994 & June 1995

Human behavior usually does not change quickly. In the event we become unconcerned, however, the words of economist Lester Thurow should shake us from our complacency:

> *No country can forever run such a huge balance of trade deficits...When the lending [to support this bad habit] stops, the dollar falls.*

But we are not helpless in dealing with this problem. The remainder of this chapter provides several actions we can take—and must take—to reverse our trade deficit.

Balance the Budget

The problems we have been discussing in this book are all interrelated. Solving one problem very often leads to at least a partial solution to another problem. This is particularly true of the trade deficit and the budget deficit.

Economists differ on their estimates of the relationship between the trade deficit and the budget deficit. Those who have tried to determine a numerical measure of the relationship have established a range between 37 percent and 55 percent. While they may not agree on a precise percentage, economists are united in saying that a big part of the trade deficit is caused by our failure to balance the federal budget. Speaking for many in his profession, economist Eric Youngkoo Lee wrote about the trade deficit, "Only cuts in the fiscal deficit should prove effective in correcting the U.S. trade imbalance." Even economist Robert Eisner, a defender of deficits, says, "Budget deficits...have contributed substantially to our large current trade deficit."

The instability of the dollar—sometimes too high and sometimes too low—has discouraged investment in U.S. plant and productive capacity, including the human part of that capacity. This leads to higher imports and a corresponding increase in the trade deficit.

Even more significant, as we will see in chapter 7, the deficit now consumes more than three-fourths of domestic savings, thereby keeping interest rates higher than they should be. This is the so-called "crowding out" theory. If the government were not borrowing money to finance the deficit, there would be less demand to borrow money. Lower demand to borrow money translates into lower interest rates.

Higher interest rates make industrial development projects more difficult to justify. For example, if a new factory cannot generate enough profit to cover the principal and interest on the funds used to build it, there is no reason to build the factory. Consequently, our rate of productivity growth is slowed.

The combination of high interest rates, instability of the dollar, and a work force that is frequently not well trained has persuaded some U.S. manufacturers to build plants in other countries where all three factors are superior—and in some cases where workers are paid less per hour than in the United States.

One of the ironies of this situation is that organized labor has opposed a balanced budget constitutional amendment. While certain unions could be hurt by a constitutional amendment because there would be cuts in government spending, the industrial unions and the construction trades have already been harmed greatly by the failure to pass the amendment. Trade deficits result in the loss of jobs in the nation running the deficit. A Brookings Institution study by Robert Lawrence found that half the loss of U.S. manufacturing jobs occurred as a result of the drop in exports from the United States and rise in imports into the United States.

As noted earlier, approximately $1.3 trillion worth of U.S. Treasury securities are now held in other countries. The interest we pay on that debt flows to those nations. The "trickle down" theory of economics holds that increased spending by the affluent will ultimately benefit everyone. While there may be a little truth to that theory within a nation, no one can make a credible case that we are ultimately helping American workers by making interest payments to wealthy citizens of Great Britain, Saudi Arabia, or Japan. Clearly, borrowing from abroad lowers our standard of living.

Having the budget in balance, except for unusual circumstances, is essential for our economic future. Economist Benjamin Friedman said:

> *One worrisome implication of America's becoming a debtor nation is simply our loss of control over our own economic policies. Losing control over one's affairs is, after all, what being in debt is all about – no less for a nation than for an individual or a business.*

Balancing the federal budget will bring us closer to eliminating the trade deficit.

Train Our Workforce Better

How many U.S.-based corporations have moved plants to other countries because of our inadequately trained workforce? No one knows, but the numbers are large. That does not mean Americans have less inherent ability than people in Japan or Germany or Taiwan or Scotland or Singapore. But privately, and sometimes publicly, industrial leaders are candid about the inadequacy of the educational background of too many Americans.

For example, at one Senate hearing, a witness told of a New England corporation that planned to build a small manufacturing plant. The choice was among Mexico, the United States, and Germany. Mexico had the advantage of the cheapest labor. The United States had the advantage of a somewhat better-prepared workforce. However, the corporation reluctantly made the decision to go to Germany, even though the average industrial wage there is now about $6.50 per hour higher than in the United States. Why? Because the German workers were much better prepared and therefore more productive for the money spent in spite of the wage differential.

A better-prepared workforce means higher productivity. Higher productivity results in a lower unit cost to manufacture an item. Lower costs increase the likelihood of successfully competing with products manufactured overseas. This leads to higher sales, which results in higher profits. Everyone wins—labor, management, stockholders, the government, and the dollar.

Build Quality Into Our Products

The surge of sales of foreign cars a decade ago occurred in part because of an overvalued dollar, but primarily because the Japanese and others were producing cars of better quality. Not too many years ago, the words *Made in Japan* signaled an inferior product. To their credit, the Japanese have completely reversed that perception. The best-selling car in the United States from 1990 to 1992 was the Honda. It was neither luck nor a snappy advertising campaign that earned Honda this distinction. It was quality manufacturing. Fortunately, American car manufacturers have learned their lesson, and they are now building quality products.

Commitment to quality does have its benefits. As recently as five years ago, the only non-luxury automobiles Americans could buy with airbags to protect both the driver and front-seat passenger were foreign-made. The U.S. government tried to push our auto manufacturers to adopt this standard, but they resisted. However, foreign manufacturers quietly incorporated this feature, providing more safety to thousands of citizens. It had the added benefit of helping sell automobiles. There are many reasons for the trade deficit, but one of the more obvious explanations is that more American citizens prefer the quality of certain foreign products to the quality of the U.S.-made counterparts.

Quality. Quality. Quality. There is no substitute for it.

Bring More Professionalism to Our Trade Negotiations

Democratic and Republican administrations have appointed excellent people from all walks of life to lead our international trade delegations. However, those officials are often new to the trade negotiation process. By the time they really understand this complex field, another president takes over, and the training process begins again. There are sectors where people without experience can work effectively, but negotiating international trade deals is not one of them.

Persuade Other Nations to Remove Non-Tariff Barriers

Tariffs are usually perceived as the major barrier to products moving from one nation to another. Where tariff barriers exist, the rates should be roughly equivalent. Where the rates are not equivalent, we should push for equality in tariff treatment. For example, before the adoption of the North American Free Trade Agreement, (on which the two authors disagree about the long-term benefits to the United States) Mexico had a tariff of 20 percent on U.S. automobiles shipped into that country, while the United States imposed only a 6 percent tariff on automobiles manufactured in Mexico that were shipped to the United States.

While tariff barriers can be significant impediments to free trade, non-tariff barriers can prove to be equally or more troublesome. For example, some of our Asian trading partners cause endless delays in approving U.S.-made products. In some cases, they virtually ban our products. Having said this, it should be added that we are dependent on some of these nations to buy our Treasury securities, and that makes it difficult to insist on changes. It is sometimes not prudent to get tough with your banker.

Become More Sensitive to Other Cultures

The Japanese, as do the British, drive on the left-hand side of the road. Therefore, for automobiles sold in Japan, the Japanese automakers build cars with the steering wheel on the right-hand side of the car. However, on automobiles bound for the United States, they place the steering wheel on the left-hand side. It would seem that U.S. automakers would reciprocate by building automobiles with right-hand steering for Japanese and British markets. But they don't!

And we handicap ourselves by persisting in using the English units of measure for most of our manufacturing processes, when almost every other industrialized nation has adopted the metric system. Not using the metric system simply makes it more difficult to sell certain products overseas.

Consider, too, that in many nations, people are accustomed to buying food products in smaller packages and quantities than we use. Sellers must learn to adapt to different markets. We must become more understanding of the cultures and buying habits of others.

Along those lines, language is another barrier our schools must help us overcome. There is an old saying, "You can buy in any language, but if you want to sell, you have to speak the language of your customer." We don't speak the languages of our customers. We lose billions of dollars every year in sales because of this deficiency. Those lost sales result in tens of thousands of lost jobs. You can't sell if you can't communicate. The United States is the only nation in the world in which a student can go through grade school, high school, and college and never study a foreign language— and we're paying for it.

Here's a terrific example of our failure to adapt to other cultures. When General Motors first produced the Chevrolet Nova, it did not sell well in Latin America. Someone finally pointed out the obvious—"*no va*" in Spanish means, "It doesn't go." GM changed the name to *Caribe*, and it sold. Someone should have recognized the problem before the Nova rolled off the production line.

Another example of our insensitivity occurred when U.S. manufacturers did not attend a specialized industrial show on water desalination equipment held in the Middle East in 1995. France and other nations were represented. "We didn't feel comfortable with the language," a U.S. industrial representative explained. That happens more often than it should.

Pay Attention to Developing Nations

Forty percent of our exports are sent to lesser-developed countries. For both economic and political reasons, we should be paying more attention to these nations. The political reason is that the great threat to the world is no longer nuclear annihilation but instability that can spill over from one nation to many nations. One way of encouraging stability is to meet the needs and hopes of people without violence. (The same is true within our own nation.) Trade is a way of helping to do that.

Foreign aid is another. After being the world leader, the United States now spends less as a percentage of its income on foreign economic assistance than any of the Western European nations or Japan. We spend less than 1 percent of our federal budget on foreign aid. Paying attention to the developing nations and their markets that will grow rapidly in the decades ahead is good for our economy and good for world stability.

Analyze Our Problems and Our Potential On an Industry-by-Industry Basis

Eighty percent of our manufacturers and contractors who could be selling abroad are not doing so. They have a vague understanding that the customers are out there, but frequently they don't know how to reach them. Seminars should be presented throughout the United States to help open this market. A few seminars are being held, but only on an extremely limited basis. Businesses that carefully explore this area often do well. The keys to success in exporting are like the keys to success in business: Be creative, work hard, and be willing to take a risk.

On another crucial front, an analysis of imports into the United States reveals that oil is our single largest problem. We are more dependent on oil imports now than during the oil shocks of the

1970s. How do we become more energy self-suffi-
cient? Should we be encouraging the development
of the electric car, now barely on the horizon?
Building homes that are "passive solar" (built with
a southern exposure to absorb heat and light) saves
huge amounts of energy. Should we be doing more
to encourage this alternative? A hundred other
questions should be asked.

However, we know we need to be much more
creative in the energy field. Former Secretary of
Commerce "Pete" Peterson has suggested that a
fifty-cent-per-gallon tax on gasoline would raise
about $50 billion, part of which could reduce the
budget deficit, help the environment, lessen our
trade deficit in oil, and still leave us with one of the
lowest gasoline taxes in the world.

The United States basically has no energy policy.
We assume that the free market system will take
care of things somehow. The reality is that energy is
an area where government and the private sector
must work together, or we will increasingly be at
the mercy of the oil-producing nations.

Agriculture is a real export success story, yet it
could become much more successful. American
farmers know how to produce food efficiently, and
the foreign markets are growing rapidly. In the
next forty-five years, the world population is
expected to double. This will create a huge

demand for food. We should plan for that situation now.

We need to identify and pursue the new opportunities for exporting our products and our know-how. The federal government can offer assistance, open doors, give encouragement, and stimulate ideas. But it's up to the private sector to take the initiative.

Stop Blaming Others for Our Failures

Does Japan have some excessively restrictive trade policies? Yes. But if every one of their unreasonable policies were dropped tomorrow, the trade pattern would not change dramatically, assuming that we would also drop our unreasonable policies. It's easy to blame others for our own failures, but it gets us nowhere. Some of the Japan-bashing, as well as references to our other trading partners, has an unhealthy tone of racism to it.

It is always easy for political leaders to make speeches condemning "those foreigners" for the loss of trade and jobs. Such speeches are usually greeted with cheers. But they do nothing to help solve the problems or even help us understand them. Yes, we must persuade other countries to be more reasonable. At the same time, we must make certain that our appointed trade representatives negotiate the best possible agreements for the United States.

Finally, we must recognize that the responsibility for our poor performance in world trade ultimately rests with us, starting with our huge federal deficit.

Examine New Tax Policies

There is currently much discussion around Capitol Hill about radically changing the U.S. tax system. However, sweeping changes should be entered into cautiously. We need stability in our tax laws and regulations. Uncertainty harms our economy and discourages investment.

Some of the leading plans and their legislative proponents are listed below.

Plan:	Sponsors:
Flat Tax	Rep. Dick Armey, R-Texas
	Sen. Richard Shelby, R-Alabama
National Sales Tax	Rep. Bill Archer, R-Texas
	Sen. Dick Lugar, R-Indiana
U.S.A. Tax Plan	Sen. Pete Domenici, R-New Mexico
	Sen. Sam Nunn, D-Georgia

Another plan worth considering has been proposed that has not received as much exposure as those listed above. Rep. Sam Gibbons, D-Florida, and Sen. Fritz Hollings, D-South Carolina, have proposed a value-added tax.

Most industrial nations have a value-added tax, which collects a small percentage at each point in the manufacturing process. The value-added tax does not apply to sales outside the manufacturing country. An advantage of this tax is that it is relatively easy to collect, and it encourages our exports, which means more jobs for the United States. Another advantage of the value-added tax is that it taxes consumption rather than savings. There seems to be growing support for a consumption-based tax system. Presumably, a value-added tax would partially or substantially replace the income tax.

The disadvantage of the value-added tax is that it is regressive. That is, everyone pays the same amount on a per-item basis. Therefore, people with smaller incomes end up paying a larger percentage of their incomes in taxes. But there are ways to compensate for that problem.

The value-added tax should be closely analyzed in connection with any plan to reform our tax system.

Putting It All Together

Just as with the budget deficit, there is no one, easy, quick answer to eliminating the trade deficit. There are, however, many policies and programs that we could undertake to reverse the trade dilemma we find ourselves in today. The changes outlined in this chapter can help us remain in a position of leadership in the world economy.

Chapter 7

Encourage Savings

n 1992, former chairman of the Council of Economic Advisors Charles Schultze observed:

The federal government cannot afford to be neutral about national savings... National savings in the United States has collapsed in recent years. The national savings rate fell from roughly 8.2 percent of national income in the period prior to 1980 to 3 percent in 1989-90.

For our purposes, national savings can simply be defined as that part of a nation's income not consumed by the private sector (individuals and companies) and the public sector (government). While the United States was saving at a rate of 3 percent, Japan saved at a rate of 17 percent, Germany saved 13 percent, and the western industrial nations averaged 12 percent, not including the United States in the calculation. At the time this book is being written, the savings rate of the United States is 3.6 percent. The graph below shows the savings rates of industrialized countries since 1980.

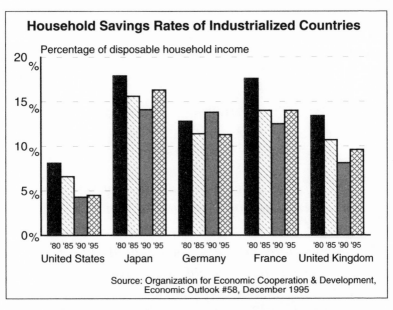

Household Savings Rates of Industrialized Countries

Percentage of disposable household income

Source: Organization for Economic Cooperation & Development, Economic Outlook #58, December 1995

The Savings Rate and the Budget Deficit

The major reason for the low savings rate of the United States is the budget deficit of the federal government. During the period from 1959 to 1980, our savings rate averaged 9.6 percent of national income. However, the federal budget deficit took 1.4 percent of that amount, so the savings rate netted 8.2 percent. If the left-hand bar in the following graph represents the total amount of money saved by Americans during the period from 1959 to 1980, then the dark portion of that bar represents the cumulative total of the budget deficits during that same period. The light portion of the bar then represents the true amount that the country, as a whole, has saved. Said yet another way, the government is just an extension of ourselves, and, therefore, when the government borrows money, it has the effect of reducing the true national savings rate of the American people.

By 1989-90, the total savings rate dropped to 6.3 percent, but the federal government took 3.3 percent of that amount, so actual savings totaled only 3 percent. The graph below clearly shows how our national savings rate is affected by continuing government deficits. Today, the federal government takes almost

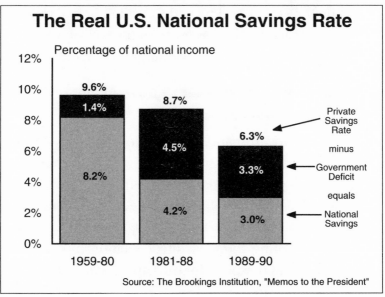

The Real U.S. National Savings Rate

Percentage of national income

Source: The Brookings Institution, "Memos to the President"

three-fourths of the nation's savings to finance the budget deficit.

The theory of the tax cut proposed by President Reagan in 1981 rested partly on the belief that if taxes were cut, people would save more. That part of the proposal seemed logical, but, in fact, people spent more and saved less. In his first televised address to the nation as president, Reagan warned viewers that he expected a deficit that year of $81 billion. He went on to add: "Can we, who man the ship of state, deny that it is somewhat out of control? Our national debt is approaching $1 trillion."

Shortly thereafter, his deficit topped $200 billion, a record-breaking figure far in excess of any previous deficits. The year he left office, the national debt not only had passed $1 trillion, it had reached $2.9 trillion. It is easy for even the well-intentioned to create debt; it is much harder to get out of it.

What Harm Is Caused by Government Consumption of Savings?

When government consumes our savings through deficit spending, there is little left for investment. Our productivity goes down, and our standard of living goes down. A study for the *Federal Reserve Bank of New York Quarterly Review* by Susan Hickok and Juann Hung found a direct relationship between savings and exports for the United States. The study also found that the Asian countries with the greatest savings growth "showed the strongest export growth over the last decade." They suggest that a 1 percent increase in savings can create an increase of 3 percent in exports. In 1980, the United States invested 16 percent of national income, but as the budget deficit went up, savings and investment went down. By 1990, investment dropped to 13.6 percent. The following graph shows this economic drop. In economic terms, that is a huge decline.

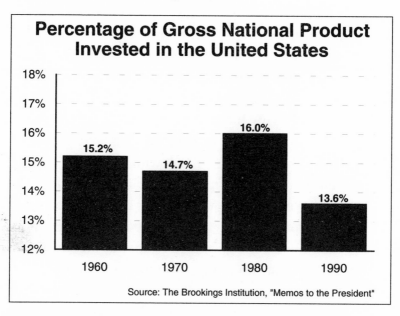

Percentage of Gross National Product Invested in the United States

Source: The Brookings Institution, "Memos to the President"

Exporting Our Goods vs. Exporting Our Money

When Americans do not save enough to meet the demands of the federal deficit and industrial investment, we borrow from other nations. This borrowing is accomplished by selling our debt securities to their governments and their citizens. Then we send interest to these nations.

A Tokyo-based economist wrote an article in an international economics magazine under the title: "America's Budget Deficits…They Redistribute Income to the Rich." He noted that the United States gets money for its huge interest payments primarily from the vast majority of middle-class, tax-paying Americans. On the other hand, the owners of the Treasury securities who are receiving the interest payments are generally more economically fortunate. Increasingly, they not only are more economically fortunate but also are living beyond our borders.

To understand more fully the extent of our dilemma, consider the following: The total interest sent to other nations from public and private borrowing exceeded $40 billion for the fiscal year ending September 30, 1995. That is one-third more than the federal government spends on education, and almost three times the amount we spend on foreign economic assistance.

Our failure to save sends interest rates higher because there are fewer dollars to meet demand. As interest rates rise, people in industry wonder whether it is profitable to modernize a plant or take other actions to make our nation more productive. People who may want to build or buy a home must determine the monthly payments they will be required to make. But their American dream is often postponed because of high interest rates. If our savings rate were higher, not only would the normal supply and demand factors operate to reduce interest rates, the Federal Reserve Board would not feel compelled to raise rates because we would be moving toward higher productivity, which lowers inflationary pressures.

The most important action we can take to increase savings is to get rid of the federal budget deficit. Economist Lester Thurow concludes: "From the point of view of long-term economic growth and international competitiveness, the federal government ought to be running a surplus and be contributing to savings rather than running a deficit and subtracting from savings."

Tax Incentives to Encourage Savings

There are some answers. The federal government can prudently make certain changes in our tax code that will encourage savings instead of debt. Today, our tax laws reward businesses that create debt to finance growth rather than financing growth through savings or equity (stock) financing. A corporation that buys another corporation by borrowing money can write off the interest payments even though the debt may create hazards for the purchasing company. But if that same corporation more prudently issues stock, the dividends are not deductible. If we changed the tax law to permit 80 percent of interest expense to be deductible and 50 percent of dividends to be deductible, the net result would be a wash in federal revenue. But many corporations would have a more solid base. Our corporate debt would decline, and we would relieve a little of the upward pressure on interest rates.

We should also discourage corporate debt for nonproductive purposes. For example, when U.S. Steel (now USX) bought Marathon Oil for $6 billion, it borrowed $4 billion of that amount. What did that do to modernize the outmoded steel plants of the nation? Nothing. How many new jobs did it create in the steel industry? None. How many new oil wells did it dig? None. What did it do to modernize Marathon's facilities? Nothing. Yet we provide tax breaks for the interest on the four billion dollars borrowed for this purpose.

Wouldn't it make more sense to give a tax break to a company that invested in research? The largest portion of each research dollar is spent on the salaries of researchers. The following graph indicates that the United States is devoting fewer of its resources to research and development efforts. In the long run, this will cripple our output as other nations bring newer and more efficient products to market.

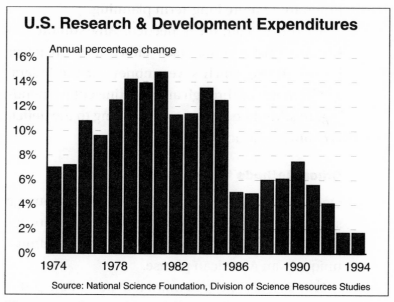

U.S. Research & Development Expenditures

Annual percentage change

Source: National Science Foundation, Division of Science Resources Studies

The tax code needs to differentiate more between productive and unproductive use of resources. Corporations should be given every incentive to spend money for the following activities:

- Research
- Plant modernization and expansion
- Worker training

Tax breaks that encourage savings by individual citizens in some cases can save the federal government more in interest than the cost of the incentive. In Germany, people who deposit savings in banks or other thrift institutions for at least seven years do not pay income tax on the interest. That encourages savings and permits the financial institution to do more long-term planning.

A word of caution is needed. Any stimulus to savings must pay for itself either through lower interest rates, which saves money for the federal government, or through an offsetting cut in spending. To stimulate savings while adding to the deficit is counterproductive.

Other Methods to Encourage Savings

One method used by many nations to encourage savings is to require higher down payments for major purchases. "No down payment" is almost uniquely an American phrase.

We must also keep in mind that part of the problem is that our culture is not as attuned to saving as it should be. Changing cultural habits will not happen in one year. But over five years, yes!

Even if public opinion cannot be completely swayed in five years, there is a compromise solution: Persuade our society to reduce its reliance upon debt. Government debt, corporate debt, and individual debt need to be addressed. The periodical, *Grant's Interest Rate Observer*, reported on September 15, 1995, that "the disparity between the growth in consumer installment debt, on the one hand, and personal income, on the other, has begun to widen again."

To the extent that this relationship reflects confidence in the future of the economy, that is a good sign. The following graph shows this in detail. But too much of an increase in any form of debt, rather than an increase in savings, is not what the nation needs.

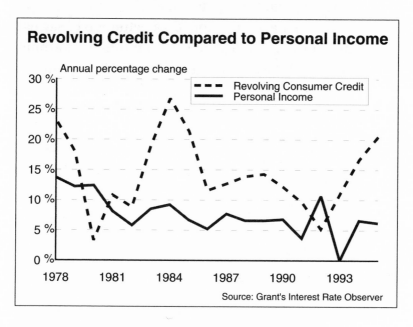

Revolving Credit Compared to Personal Income

Annual percentage change

- - - Revolving Consumer Credit
Personal Income

Source: Grant's Interest Rate Observer

In 1988, Sen. Daniel Patrick Moynihan wrote:

We are consuming too much and saving too little. We have a lower rate of investment than any of our competitors, save Great Britain. The average age of machinery in our factories is twice that of Japan...We are now saving 5 percent of income. Saving 6 percent won't change a thing. It's time to set our minds on 20 percent.

Three years later, our net savings stood at 2.3 percent, lower than Britain's 2.7 percent, Japan's 20.4 percent, Germany's 9.9 percent, France's 7.5 percent, and Italy's 6.7 percent.

Unless we, as a nation, do a better job of saving, our currency is destined to continue its downhill slide, and it will take our standard of living with it.

Chapter 8

Think Long Term

The United States needs to look for solid, long-term answers, not quick solutions. Unfortunately, our society is geared to look for the latter, both in political life and in business. "How will this play in the next election?" and, "What will this do to next quarter's earnings?" seem to be the most important questions in politics and business, respectively. We are less inclined to ask, "If we follow this policy, where will we be in ten years?"

The correct, long-term answers will not come from polling or from focus groups, but from leadership that has carefully studied the experience of the United States and other nations through the centuries. Political leaders can become as addicted to polls as junkies become addicted to illegal drugs. The results can be almost as ruinous.

To solve the dollar problem and get the United States back to its position of economic and political leadership, we need well-reasoned solutions that will serve not only the immediate audience but also future generations. For example, when New Zealand adopted a monetary policy with the clear objective of lowering its inflation rate to between zero and 2 percent, a very positive impact occurred with respect to the currency as well as investment in the country.

The United States is still the only nation that can provide effective international leadership. We should do it. We must work with other nations, but we must also lead. Leadership means more than bluster. We cannot do as one former cabinet member did at one financial summit meeting, when he told the other participants, "The dollar may be our currency, but it's your problem."

Manipulation by key leaders of the dollar or yen or deutsche mark or other currencies can have a short-term effect and a limited longer impact. However, our goal should be the long-term stability of the dollar, not volatility of the type we witness after a statement by the president or secretary of the Treasury or chairman of the Federal Reserve Board.

As noted earlier, the 1985 meeting at the Plaza Hotel in New York of the financial leaders of the seven major industrialized nations, called by then Treasury Secretary James Baker, did cause a change in the status of the dollar. He pressured the other nations to lower the value of the dollar to help the U.S. balance of trade. Known as *The Plaza Accord*, the pact did lower the value of the dollar, but whether the long-term results helped or hurt the United States is still a matter of dispute.

What is not in dispute is that if the United States will pay more attention to the underlying causes of the excessive increases or decreases in the value of the dollar, the entire world will benefit—and particularly the United States. The first result will be that accords to stabilize the dollar will not be needed as often. The second result will be that when accords are needed, they should be more easily and effectively implemented.

To get the dollar in better shape, we must follow the steps outlined in the previous chapters, particularly passing a balanced budget amendment to the Constitution. Unless we get our fiscal house in order on a permanent basis, our actions will be an embarrassment when viewed by coming generations.

Stability Through Intervention

Once the underlying causes of our currency problems are addressed, the United States should join with Japan and Germany and a few other nations with sound currencies in a statement that the dollar (or other currencies in the agreement) will be permitted to go up or down within certain publicly specified limits. Whenever those limits are exceeded, the central banks will agree to enter the market to stabilize the currency. Economist Charles Schultze is on solid ground when he says: "It would be wise to discount the possibility of exchange intervention alone to bring about large and lasting changes in a currency's value...Intervention may prove useful when employed with other, more basic policy changes."

When an overvalued currency declines in value, it is likely to fall farther than it should, and in that type of situation intervention will be helpful. A 1993 study by Kathryn Dominguez and Jeffrey Frankel for the Institute for International Economics suggested that when there is intervention, it should be done publicly. They concluded:

> *If, as our results suggest, intervention has an important effect on the exchange rates only when it influences expectations, this implies that the intervention must be publicly known in order to be effective. It follows that, contrary to much actual practice, the authorities should make their intervention activities public.*

The document agreed upon by the European Community for a common currency in 1999 calls for the nations involved to "respect the normal fluctuation margins," and suggests, but does not specifically require, that there could be a 2.25 percent margin or fluctuation before intervention would be initiated.

The central bankers could then meet once a year to deal with other nations that might want to be part of an accord to make such modifications as necessary, though modifications should be rare. The objective should be a solid, stable currency with careful limits on growth tied to productivity. A stable currency will bring increased investments that add to the productivity and standard of living of people everywhere. Investors, other than currency traders, usually do not like to gamble on what might happen to a currency. The United States and the world need calm in the currency markets.

Beyond Intervention

However, more than fiscal prudence is needed. We recommend that after the 1996 presidential election, the president and key members of his administration join the chairman of the Federal Reserve Board and the leadership of both parties in Congress in developing a domestic investment program that would serve as a financial mission statement for the country. The American public certainly will applaud such a plan because it would, for the first time, provide an economic blueprint for the next century.

Many components of such a plan have been discussed in this book. In addition, to build the financial base of the nation, we also must address at last three factors that retard our productive capacity:

- Education
- Research
- Poverty

Education

Education is listed first because it must be given the highest priority. We cannot afford "more of the same." Much that is happening in our schools is good, but too many young people graduate from high school without having been challenged, and often without having acquired the basic literacy and math skills everyone needs. The overwhelming reason for our high standard of living—and that of other industrialized nations—is our investment in people, an investment that produces our intellectual base.

The United States is ahead of all other nations in higher education, though the gap is narrowing. But in elementary and high school education, we are lagging. No matter who is elected as the next president, no matter who is elected to the Senate and House, one trend is not going to change: The demand for unskilled labor is declining. Yet too many young people leave school untrained, although few of them are untrainable.

We need to be more creative, and we need to draw greater numbers of parents into the education process. And when we encounter parents who lack basic literacy or are severely limited, we should seize the opportunity to train them so the problem is not compounded. Sometimes crime and drugs and alcohol are the dead ends for parents and students who have no hope, who have given up. We must give them hope, which can come in the form of increased cooperation between schools and businesses. For example, the School-to-Work program should be expanded.

We should persuade religious groups and community organizations to enlist volunteers to work one-on-one with students who need help and who need to know that someone cares about them.

At all levels of government, we should reexamine what we accept as part of our education culture. For example, our children attend elementary and high school for 180 days a year, while their counterparts in Japan and Germany attend school for 243 days and 240 days, respectively. Can our children learn as much in 180 days as their children learn in 240 days? To ask the question is to answer it. If we were to increase our school year from 180 days to 210 days—still behind many nations—that would be the equivalent of two more years of school by the time a student finishes the twelfth grade.

Why do we have a school year of 180 days? It is a relic of our predominantly agrarian past. In theory, children can still go out and harvest the crops because they are not required to be in school during the summer. Even in rural Makanda, Illinois (population 402), or Prosper, Texas (population 619), there aren't many children harvesting crops these days. Our society and our world have changed, but our form of education has not, and it must.

It also is of no small significance that of those in our prisons today—including local jails—82 percent are high school dropouts. If we want a strong anti-crime program, we must do a better job of educating the populace, particularly in the inner cities and rural areas.

Improving the education of our children is vitally important, but because new workers only account for 2 to 3 percent of the work force each year, we must understand that such an effort will not have an immediate impact upon our productivity. Therefore, it is logical that we need to improve the skills of our already existing labor force. We must encourage adults to add to their capabilities and to further their education. In particular, we should promote a major drive to end adult illiteracy. The extent of that problem is stunning. Approximately 23 million adult Americans cannot read a newspaper or complete a job application properly. This is a huge drain on the resources of our nation.

Compounding the adult illiteracy crisis is the knowledge that children in a home where the parent or parents cannot read and write are likely to perform poorly in school, and many will become high school dropouts. And adults who have extremely limited skills are more likely to be unemployed. A hopeful sign is the discovery that a few third-world nations have been able to improve their adult literacy rates dramatically within just a few years. There is nothing to prevent the United States from doing the same. We can wait no longer.

Research

The second significant factor impeding the productive capacity of the United States is the lack of resources devoted to research. Germany and Japan are far ahead of us on non-defense research, and they are probably even farther ahead in applying it to productive purposes.

In some fields, such as health research, we are the leaders, although even there much more could be done. In military defense developments we are far ahead—and we want to stay there—but most of our spending in this field does little to enhance our standard of living. The Japanese surpass us in producing better television sets, but we are ahead of them in developing nuclear missiles. We all have neighbors who buy television sets. Not too many of us have neighbors who are shopping for nuclear missiles.

The United States needs to place greater emphasis on research that adds to our quality of life and has commercial value as well. The federal government could greatly facilitate this effort by the spending priorities it sets each year. In addition, it could encourage additional private sector research through modest changes in the tax laws.

Poverty

A third major problem that retards our economy is poverty. A shocking 24 percent of our children live in poverty. **No other western industrialized nation has a poverty rate anywhere close to that stunning figure**. This is more than ten times the rate of some nations. This 24 percent statistic is not an act of God but the result of flawed policy.

Reducing this percentage—so that more members of our population are able to add to the economy instead of taking from it—will not be easy. But historians are likely to look back on those who live and lead today and judge them to a great extent by their response to this critical need. Education is part of the answer. Determining how people can be transformed into productive citizens, despite severe skill limitations, must be a part of that equation. The nation did it with the Works Progress Administration half a century ago. It would certainly seem that creative, sensitive people of today should be able to find more sensible answers than putting people onto the welfare rolls.

People who are simply handed a check for doing nothing are robbed of pride. They do not have the inner satisfaction that comes with contributing something of themselves to society. They have no infrastructure that tells them their existence is meaningful.

As an added incentive, finding work-related answers to the welfare problem might also produce answers to the crime problem. The highest rate of unemployment is among young males, and they also represent the group committing the most crimes. It is no accident that any area of high unemployment—African-American, Hispanic or white—is also an area of high crime. That does not excuse the crime, but if responsible and caring citizens develop job alternatives to unemployment, the crime problem that plagues our nation can be substantially reduced.

This book has discussed four areas of concern facing the United States:

- Stabilizing the dollar
- Improving education
- Promoting research
- Reducing poverty

The first item was the primary subject of this book, but the other three are equally important. One further observation about those four areas is warranted. The increasing level of partisanship in government will do nothing to solve these problems. During the years that the two authors have observed the political scene, much that is good has been achieved. But the growing tendency by both Democrats and Republicans toward excessive partisanship has made resolving serious problems more difficult. It has reduced the public's faith in government, and it has diminished confidence in the two major political parties. People ordinarily are elected with a political label, and they should be proud of their affiliation. But once elections are over, generally there are not Democratic or Republican answers to problems. Instead, there are realistic answers that should be pursued by committed men and women working together. Less political posturing and more determination to resolve problems in a nonpartisan manner certainly would raise the public's esteem for officeholders and our system of government.

The need to stabilize the dollar cannot be over-stated. The last three items listed at the top of the previous page are dependent upon a strong, stable dollar. Without it, there are not enough resources to fight and win those three battles. There is no question that we have the ability to solve these problems and to lift ourselves by our own bootstraps. **The only question that remains is, "Do we have the will?"**

Chapter 9

A Conclusion
That Needs You

I f, after reading this message, you put it down and say, "Fine book," but do nothing more, then the authors have not succeeded. America needs citizens who are concerned and will follow through on their concerns. If you were asked whether you are patriotic, you would reply, "Yes." But sensible patriotism sometimes demands actions other than putting on a uniform for our country. President Grover Cleveland, in 1892, put it this way, "Patriotism is no substitute for a sound currency."

We have covered a lot of ground in this book. First, we explained the creation and development of currencies and the difficulties that can arise if they are not properly managed. Next, we looked at the danger that current policies pose for the United States, its economy, and its citizens, both current and future. Finally, we proposed what can be done—and must be done—to prevent the inappropriate policies of today from robbing our children of the blessings this great country has provided her citizens over the last two centuries. Now it's time to consider which specific steps each citizen can take to help win the serious battle we currently face.

We need your help to have sensible patriotism—not just empty flag-waving—and a sound currency.

Here are five things you can do:

1. Contact six of your friends who might be interested in the subjects we have discussed. Have them come to your home, or meet them at a restaurant, or in your office. Tell them of your concerns and say, "We ought to do something." Discuss what you can and should do. Be creative. Brainstorm. During the course of the discussion, you may develop eight or nine ideas with limited merit, but you will discover at least one or two with real potential on which you can act.

2. Write to your U.S. representatives and U.S. senators at the addresses below. If there is a campaign in progress when you read this, contact the candidates. Tell them about one or two suggestions in this book—or of your own that you hope they will act on.

Representative_____   Senator_____
Washington, D.C. 20515   Washington, D.C. 20510

3. Read more and learn more. We have discussed complicated issues, but the big problem is not their complexity. The true difficulty is finding the political courage required to advocate the answers necessary to solve the problems. Let officeholders and candidates know that you are looking for solid solutions, not easy answers.

4. When you feel comfortable enough about what needs to be done, send a letter to the editor of your local newspaper. Most people are unaware that letters to the editor are read more than the newspaper's editorials. You can influence others.

5. Plan a program for one of the many civic clubs in your town or in your area. Most organizations are eager for such presentations.

There is one last request. After acting on some of these suggestions, go to your calendar and make a note on the date two months from today—a note that tells you to follow through on these items. Then go to the last page in your calendar and write: "I helped to change history."

Index